Morgan

DIANE LINDSEY REEVES

Illustrations by
NANCY BOND

Checkmark Books™

An imprint of Facts On File, Inc.

CAREER IDEAS FOR KIDS WHO LIKE SCIENCE

Copyright © 1998 by Diane Lindsey Reeves

Checkmark Books
An imprint of Facts On File, Inc.
11 Penn Plaza
New York NY 10001

Library of Congress Cataloging-in-Publication Data
Reeves, Diane Lindsey, 1959–
    Science / Diane Lindsey Reeves.
        p.   cm.—(Career ideas for kids who like)
    Summary: Provides activities to uncover individual traits and
abilities, information about careers in science, description of career
planning resources, explanations for personal roadmaps, and profiles
of individual scientists.
    ISBN 0-8160-3680-2 (hardcover).—ISBN 0-8160-3686-1 (pbk.)
    1. Science—Vocational guidance—Juvenile literature.
    [1. Science—Vocational guidance. 2. Vocational guidance.]
    I. Title.   II. Series: Reeves, Diane Lindsey, 1959–   Career ideas for
kids who like.
    Q147.R38   1998
    502'.3—dc21   97-37048

Checkmark Books are available at special discounts when purchased in
quantities for businesses, associations, institutions or sales promotions.
Please call our Special Sales Department in New York at 212/967-8800 ‹
800/322-8755.

You can find Facts On File on the World Wide Web at http://www.factsonfile.

Text and cover design by Smart Graphics
Illustrations by Nancy Bond

This book is printed on acid-free paper.

Printed in the United States of America

MP FOF 10 9 8 7 6 5 4 3 2 1

(pbk)   10 9 8 7 6 5 4 3 2 1

To my daughters,
Lindsey Leilani and Lacey Rochelle,
the inspiration behind these books.
Each page is filled with my love and hopes
for your both finding your
special place in the world.

CONTENTS

Acknowledgments		ix
Make a Choice!		1
	Choice A	1
	Choice B	2
How to Use This Book		3
Get in Gear!		7
	Watch for Signs Along the Way	7
	Get Some Direction	9
	Calculate the Clues	14
Take a Trip!		17
	Archaeologist	19
	Astronomer	27
	Chemist	34
	Engineer	40
	Food Scientist	48
	Horticulturist	54
	Landscape Architect	62
	Medical Technologist	68
	Meteorologist	74
	Nutritionist	81
	Oceanographer	87
	Pharmacist	96
	Robotics Technician	105
	Science Educator	111
	Veterinarian	119

Make a Scientific Detour! **127**
  A World of Science Careers 128
  Information Is Power 132

Don't Stop Now! **135**
  #1 Narrow Down Your Choices 137
  #2 Snoop at the Library 137
  #3 Chat on the Phone 139
  #4 Surf the Net 141
  #5 Shadow a Professional 143

What's Next? **147**
  Red Light 148
  Yellow Light 149
  Green Light 150

Hooray! You Did It! **153**

Some Future Destinations **155**
  It's Not Just for Nerds 156
  Awesome Internet Career Resources 156
  It's Not Just for Boys 157
  More Career Books Especially
    for the Scientifically Inclined 157
  Heavy-Duty Resources 158
  Finding Places to Work 158
  Finding Places to Practice Job Skills 159
  No-College Occupations 160

  Index **161**

ACKNOWLEDGMENTS

A million thanks to the people who took the time to share
their career stories and provide photos for this book:

Gibor Basri
Michael Blackwell
Leslie Bonci
Anthony Conte
Carol Ellick
Al Kaltenback
Henry Lee
Richard Lefebvre
Rose Lindsey
Ellen Molner
John Morales
Julius Nuccio
Ben Page
Greg Socha
Steve Spangler

Also, special thanks to the design team of Smart Graphics,
Nancy Bond, and Cathy Rincon for bringing the
Career Ideas for Kids series to life with their creative talent.

Finally, much appreciation and admiration is due to
my editor, Nicole Bowen, whose vision and attention
to detail increased the quality of this project in
many wonderful ways.

MAKE A CHOICE!

You're young. Most of your life is still ahead of you. How are you supposed to know what you want to be when you grow up?

You're right: 10, 11, 12, 13, is a bit young to know exactly what and where and how you're going to do whatever it is you're going to do as an adult. But, it's the perfect time to start making some important discoveries about who you are, what you like to do, and what you do best. It's the ideal time to start thinking about what you *want* to do.

Make a choice! If you get a head start now, you may avoid setbacks and mistakes later on.

When it comes to picking a career, you've basically got two choices.

CHOICE A

Wait until you're in college to start figuring out what you want to do. Even then you still may not decide what's up your alley, so you graduate and jump from job to job still searching for something you really like.

Hey, it could work. It might be fun. Lots of (probably most) people do it this way.

The problem is that if you pick Choice A, you may end up settling for second best. You may miss out on a meaningful education, satisfying work, and the rewards of a focused and well-planned career.

You have another choice to consider.

CHOICE B

Start now figuring out your options and thinking about the things that are most important in your life's work: Serving others? Staying true to your values? Making lots of money? Enjoying your work? Your young years are the perfect time to mess around with different career ideas without messing up your life.

Reading this book is a great idea for kids who choose B. It's a first step toward choosing a career that matches your skills, interests, and lifetime goals. It will help you make a plan for tailoring your junior and high school years to fit your career dreams. To borrow a jingle from the U.S. Army—using this book is a way to discover how to "be all that you can be."

Ready for the challenge of Choice B? If so, read the next section to find out how this book can help start you on your way.

HOW TO USE THIS BOOK

This isn't a book about interesting careers that other people have. It's a book about interesting careers that you can have.

Of course, it won't do you a bit of good to just read this book. To get the whole shebang, you're going to have to jump in with both feet, roll up your sleeves, put on your thinking cap—whatever it takes—to help you do these three things:

- 💡 **Discover** what you do best and enjoy the most. (This is the secret ingredient for finding work that's perfect for you.)

   ☆ **Explore** ways to match your interests and abilities with career ideas.

   ☆ **Experiment** with lots of different ideas until you find the ideal career. (It's like trying on all kinds of hats to see which ones fit!)

Use this book as a road map to some exciting career destinations. Here's what to expect in the chapters that follow.

GET IN GEAR!

First stop: self-discovery. These activities will help you uncover important clues about the special traits and abilities that make you *you*. When you are finished you will have developed a personal Skill Set that will help guide you to career ideas in the next chapter.

TAKE A TRIP!

Next stop: exploration. Cruise down the career idea highway and find out about a variety of career ideas that are especially appropriate for people who like science. Use the Skill Set chart at the beginning of each entry to match your own interests with those required for success on the job.

MAKE A SCIENTIFIC DETOUR!

Here's your chance to explore up-and-coming opportunities in environmental and technology sciences as well as the tried-and-true fields of research, medicine, and basic, hard-core sciences.

Just when you thought you'd seen it all, here come dozens of interesting science ideas to add to the career mix. Charge up your career search by learning all you can about some of these opportunities.

DON'T STOP NOW!

Third stop: experimentation. The library, the telephone, a computer, and a mentor—four keys to a successful career planning adventure. Use them well, and before long you'll be on the trail of some hot career ideas.

WHAT'S NEXT?

Make a plan! Chart your course (or at least the next stop) with these career planning road maps. Whether you're moving full steam ahead with a great idea or get slowed down at a yellow light of indecision, these road maps will keep you moving forward toward a great future.

Use a pencil—you're bound to make a detour or two along the way. But, hey, you've got to start somewhere.

HOORAY! YOU DID IT!

Some final rules of the road before sending you off to new adventures.

SOME FUTURE DESTINATIONS

This section lists a few career planning tools you'll want to know about.

You've got a lot of ground to cover in this phase of your career planning journey. Start your engines and get ready for an exciting adventure!

GET IN GEAR!

Career planning is a lifelong journey. There's usually more than one way to get where you're going, and there are often some interesting detours along the way. But, you have to start somewhere. So, rev up and find out all you can about you—one-of-a-kind, specially designed you. That's the first stop on what can be the most exciting trip of your life!

To get started, complete the two exercises described below.

WATCH FOR SIGNS ALONG THE WAY

Road signs help drivers figure out how to get where they want to go. They provide clues about direction, road conditions, and safety. Your career road signs will provide clues about who you are, what you like, and what you do best. These clues can help you decide where to look for the career ideas that are best for you.

Complete the following statements to make them true for you. There are no right or wrong answers. Jot down the response that describes you best. Your answers will provide important clues about career paths you should explore.

Please Note: If this book does not belong to you, write your responses on a separate sheet of paper.

On my last report card, I got the best grade in _____.

On my last report card, I got the worst grade in _____.

I am happiest when _____.

Something I can do for hours without getting bored is _____.

Something that bores me out of my mind is _____.

My favorite class is _____.

My least favorite class is _____.

The one thing I'd like to accomplish with my life is _____.

My favorite thing to do after school is _____.

My least favorite thing to do after school is _____.

Something I'm really good at is _____.

Something that is really tough for me to do is _____.

My favorite adult person is _____ because _____.

When I grow up _____.

The kinds of books I like to read are about _____.

The kinds of videos I like to watch are about _____.

GET SOME DIRECTION

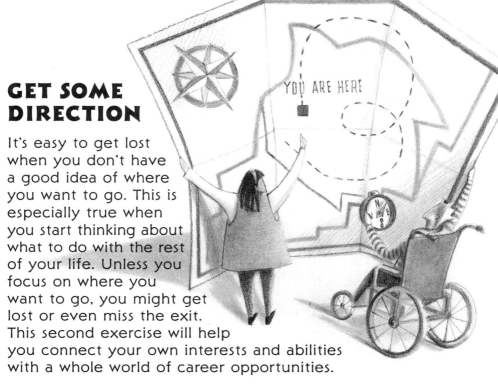

It's easy to get lost when you don't have a good idea of where you want to go. This is especially true when you start thinking about what to do with the rest of your life. Unless you focus on where you want to go, you might get lost or even miss the exit. This second exercise will help you connect your own interests and abilities with a whole world of career opportunities.

Mark the activities that you enjoy doing or would enjoy doing if you had the chance. Be picky. Don't mark ideas that you wish you would do, mark only those that you would really do. For instance, if the idea of skydiving sounds appealing, but you'd never do it because you are terrified of heights, don't mark it.

Please Note: If this book does not belong to you, write your responses on a separate sheet of paper.

❑ 1. Rescue a cat stuck in a tree
❑ 2. Paint a mural on the cafeteria wall
❑ 3. Run for student council
❑ 4. Send e-mail to a "pen pal" in another state
❑ 5. Find out all there is to know about the American Revolution
❑ 6. Survey your classmates to find out what they do after school
❑ 7. Try out for the school play
❑ 8. Dissect a frog and identify the different organs
❑ 9. Play baseball, soccer, football or _____ (fill in your favorite sport)

❑ 10. Talk on the phone to just about anyone who will talk back

❑ 11. Try foods from all over the world—Thailand, Poland, Japan, etc.

❑ 12. Write poems about things that are happening in your life

❑ 13. Create a really scary haunted house to take your friends through on Halloween

❑ 14. Bake a cake and decorate it for your best friend's birthday

❑ 15. Sell enough advertisements for the school yearbook to win a trip to Walt Disney World

❑ 16. Simulate an imaginary flight through space on your computer screen

❑ 17. Collect stamps, coins, baseball cards, or whatever and organize them into a fancy display

❑ 18. Build model airplanes, boats, doll houses, or anything from kits

❑ 19. Teach your friends a new dance routine

❑ 20. Watch the stars come out at night and see how many constellations you can find

❑ 21. Watch baseball, soccer, football or _____ (fill in your favorite sport) on TV

❑ 22. Give a speech in front of the entire school

❑ 23. Plan the class field trip to Washington, D.C.

❑ 24. Read everything in sight, including the back of the cereal box

❑ 25. Figure out "who dunnit" in a mystery story

❑ 26. Make a poster announcing the school football game

❑ 27. Think up a new way to make the lunch line move faster and explain it to the cafeteria staff

❑ 28. Put together a multimedia show for a school assembly using music and lots of pictures and graphics

❑ 29. Visit historic landmarks like the Statue of Liberty and Civil War battlegrounds

❑ 30. Invest your allowance in the stock market and keep track of how it does

❑ 31. Go to the ballet or opera every time you get the chance

❏ 32. Do experiments with a chemistry set
❏ 33. Keep score at your sister's Little League game
❏ 34. Use lots of funny voices when reading stories to children
❏ 35. Ride on airplanes, trains, boats—anything that moves
❏ 36. Interview the new exchange student for an article in the school newspaper
❏ 37. Build your own treehouse
❏ 38. Visit an art museum and pick out your favorite painting
❏ 39. Play Monopoly® in an all-night championship challenge
❏ 40. Make a chart on the computer to show how much soda students buy from the school vending machines each week
❏ 41. Find out all you can about your family ancestors and make a family tree
❏ 42. Keep track of how much your team earns to buy new uniforms
❏ 43. Play an instrument in the school band or orchestra
❏ 44. Put together a 1,000-piece puzzle
❏ 45. Write stories about sports for the school newspaper
❏ 46. Listen to other people talk about their problems
❏ 47. Imagine yourself in exotic places

❏ 48. Hang around bookstores and libraries
❏ 49. Play harmless practical jokes on April Fools' Day
❏ 50. Take photographs at the school talent show
❏ 51. Make money by setting up your own business—paper route, lemonade stand, etc.
❏ 52. Create an imaginary city using a computer
❏ 53. Look for Native American artifacts and arrowheads
❏ 54. Do 3-D puzzles
❏ 55. Keep track of the top 10 songs of the week
❏ 56. Train your dog to do tricks
❏ 57. Make play-by-play announcements at the school football game
❏ 58. Answer the phones during a telethon to raise money for orphans
❏ 59. Be an exchange student in another country
❏ 60. Write down all your secret thoughts and favorite sayings in a journal
❏ 61. Jump out of an airplane (with a parachute, of course)
❏ 62. Use a video camera to make your own movies
❏ 63. Get your friends together to help clean up your town after a hurricane
❏ 64. Spend your summer at a computer camp learning lots of new computer programs

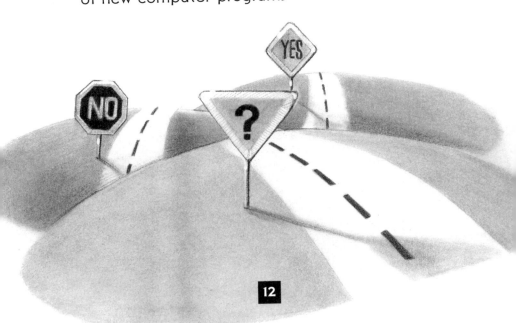

❏ 65. Help your little brother or sister make ink out of blueberry juice

❏ 66. Build bridges, sky-scrapers, and other structures out of LEGO®s

❏ 67. Plan a concert in the park for little kids

❏ 68. Collect different kinds of rocks

❏ 69. Help plan a sports tournament

❏ 70. Be DJ for the school dance

❏ 71. Learn how to fly a plane or sail a boat

❏ 72. Write funny captions for pictures in the school year-book

❏ 73. Scuba dive to search for buried treasure

❏ 74. Sketch pictures of your friends

❏ 75. Pick out neat stuff to sell at the school store

❏ 76. Answer your classmates' questions about how to use the computer

❏ 77. Make a timeline showing important things that hap-pened during the year

❏ 78. Draw a map showing how to get to your house from school

❏ 79. Make up new words to your favorite songs

❏ 80. Take a hike and name the different kinds of trees, birds, or flowers

❏ 81. Referee intramural basketball games

❏ 82. Join the school debate team

❏ 83. Make a poster with postcards from all the places you went on your summer vacation

❏ 84. Write down stories that your grandparents tell you about when they were young

CALCULATE THE CLUES

Now is your chance to add it all up. Each of the 12 boxes on these pages contains an interest area that is common to both your world and the world of work. Follow these directions to discover your personal Skill Set:

1. Find all of the numbers that you checked on pages 9–13 in the boxes below and X them. Work your way all the way through number 84.
2. Go back and count the Xs marked for each interest area. Write that number in the space that says "total."
3. Find the interest area with the highest total and put a number one in the "Rank" blank of that box. Repeat this process for the next two highest scoring areas. Rank the second highest as number two and the third highest as number three.
4. If you have more than three strong areas, choose the three that are most important and interesting to you.

Remember: If this book does not belong to you, write your responses on a separate sheet of paper.

ADVENTURE

❑ 1
❑ 13
❑ 25
❑ 37
❑ 49
❑ 61
❑ 73
Total: _____
Rank: _____

ART

❑ 2
❑ 14
❑ 26
❑ 38
❑ 50
❑ 62
❑ 74
Total: _____
Rank: _____

BUSINESS

❑ 3
❑ 15
❑ 27
❑ 39
❑ 51
❑ 63
❑ 75
Total: _____
Rank: _____

COMPUTERS

❏ 4
❏ 16
❏ 28
❏ 40
❏ 52
❏ 64
❏ 76
Total: _____
Rank: _____

HISTORY

❏ 5
❏ 17
❏ 29
❏ 41
❏ 53
❏ 65
❏ 77
Total: _____
Rank: _____

MATH

❏ 6
❏ 18
❏ 30
❏ 42
❏ 54
❏ 66
❏ 78
Total: _____
Rank: _____

MUSIC/DANCE

❏ 7
❏ 19
❏ 31
❏ 43
❏ 55
❏ 67
❏ 79
Total: _____
Rank: _____

SCIENCE

❏ 8
❏ 20
❏ 32
❏ 44
❏ 56
❏ 68
❏ 80
Total: _____
Rank: _____

SPORTS

❏ 9
❏ 21
❏ 33
❏ 45
❏ 57
❏ 69
❏ 81
Total: _____
Rank: _____

TALKING

❏ 10
❏ 22
❏ 34
❏ 46
❏ 58
❏ 70
❏ 82
Total: _____
Rank: _____

TRAVEL

❏ 11
❏ 23
❏ 35
❏ 47
❏ 59
❏ 71
❏ 83
Total: _____
Rank: _____

WRITING

❏ 12
❏ 24
❏ 36
❏ 48
❏ 60
❏ 72
❏ 84
Total: _____
Rank: _____

What are your top three interest areas? List them here (or on a separate piece of paper).

1. _____

2. _____

3. _____

This is your personal Skill Set and provides important clues about the kinds of work you're most likely to enjoy. Remember it and look for career ideas with a skill set that matches yours most closely.

TAKE A TRIP!

Cruise down the career idea highway and enjoy in-depth profiles of some of the interesting options in this field. Keep in mind all that you've discovered about yourself so far. Find the careers that match your own Skill Set first. After that, keep on trucking through the other ideas—exploration is the name of this game.

You'll probably notice that many of the careers in this book require a combined knowledge of science and math. That's because math is the language of science. If you don't know math, you can't "speak" science. If a scientific field is in your future, count on taking some fairly heavy-duty math courses, too. Add this element to the equation as you start your trip down Scientific Opportunity Avenue.

You may also notice that many of these professions require college degrees, master's degrees, or higher. Education, and plenty of it, is one of the main routes to many traditional scientific careers. It makes sense that in a field based on many complex, unchangeable laws, the more you know about the laws, the more you can do in the field.

However, if you love science but don't love the idea of spending years in school, don't despair! There's usually more than one way to get just about anywhere. Sometimes you just have to be a little more creative.

One path to a scientific career without a college degree leads to a single word: *technician*. Behind every full-fledged scientist is a good technician assisting in a variety of interesting and invaluable ways. Make technician your final destination or a pitstop on the way to other things.

Meanwhile, as you read about the following careers, imagine yourself doing each job and ask yourself the following questions:

☀ Would I like it?
☀ Would I be good at it?
☀ Is it the stuff my career dreams are made of?

If so, make a quick exit to explore what it involves, try it out, check it out, and get acquainted.

Buckle up and enjoy the trip!

Archaeologist

SKILL SET

✔ SCIENCE

✔ HISTORY

✔ TRAVEL

GO visit natural history museums.

READ *National Geographic* magazines.

TRY investigating the past—dig up all the information you can about Native Americans, the Aztecs, early American settlers, or another group of interest.

WHAT IS AN ARCHAEOLOGIST?

An archaeologist is part researcher, part historian, part investigator. He or she must be handy with a shovel and pick. These are the bare bones basics of an archaeologist's work. Archaeologists gather information and recover data that link the past with the present. Everything they do centers around answering three questions about the peo-ple who once inhabited each excavation site: Who lived here? How did they live? What was life like?

Archaeology is actually a subfield of anthropology. While archaeology is the study of what people leave behind, anthro-pology is the study of people and their

behavior. Three other subfields combine to create a full pic-ture of life in the past. One of these is linguistics—the study of language; another is physical anthropology—the study of human remains; and the third one is cultural anthropology—the study of modern-day cultures and peoples.

All four disciplines fit together like pieces of a puzzle. Scientists generally specialize in one area and work with col-legues of the other areas to make well-rounded conclusions about their findings. Count on all four areas being part of your course of study if you pursue either the field of archae-ology or the field of anthropology.

Archaeology is the systematic recovery of evidence of human life in the past. Physical objects or artifacts such as art and tools provide clues about life as it used to be. An archae-ologist researches, excavates, preserves, studies, and classifies artifacts to develop a picture of how people lived in earlier cultures and societies.

Archaeological fieldwork is conducted all over the world, often in remote areas, and can be as diverse in nature as tracing the paths of ancient hunter-gatherers or reconstruct-ing the lives and times of early American settlers. Recovering this data can be a painstaking process as these historic finds are often deeply buried in the ground, covered by later civ-ilizations. Archaeologists work carefully and skillfully to remove objects and record their relationship to each other. A thorough cleaning, cataloging, and analysis is systematical-ly conducted on each object as archaeologists figure out how to fit their findings into the broad scheme of human history.

Many archaeologists are employed at colleges and univer-sities and teach at least part-time between projects. Others work for government agencies such as the U.S. Forest Service or for private industry. Archaeology is a relatively small field with professionals marked by a common passion for making new discoveries. Those who continue to thrive (that is, "make a good living") in this field are the ones who find creative ways to combine their interest in archaeology with other skills in greater demand (see the Get Acquainted profile for a great example of this).

TRY IT OUT

READ ALL ABOUT IT

The following list consists of some interesting books that provide an overview of archaeology.

Anderson, Joan. *From Map to Museum*. New York: Morrow Junior Books, 1988.

Ballard, Robert D. *Exploring the Titanic*. Toronto: Madison Press, 1988.

Caselli, Giovanni. *History and Everyday Things*. New York: Peter Bedrick, 1983.

Ceram, C. W. *Gods, Graves and Scholars: The Story of Archaeology*. New York: Vintage Books, 1986.

Cook, Barbara, and Sturand Reid. *The Young Scientist Book of Archeology*. Tulsa, Okla.: EDC Publishing, 1987.

Corbishley, Mike. *Time Detectives: Secret Cities*. New York: E. P. Dutton, Lodestar Books, 1989.

Fagan, Brian M. *The Adventure of Archeology*. Washington, D.C.: National Geographic Society, 1989.

Gallant, Roy A. *Lost Cities*. New York: Franklin Watts, 1985.

Macaulay, David. *Motel of the Mysteries*. Boston: Houghton Mifflin, 1979.

McIntosh, Jane. *The Practical Archaeologist*. New York: Facts On File, 1986.

Porell, Bruce. *Digging the Past: Archaeology in Your Own Backyard*. Reading, Mass.: Addison-Wesley, 1979.

The latest and greatest in archaeological discoveries are often as close as the nearest magazine rack. Curl up in a cozy chair and escape to worlds newly discovered.

🔅 *National Geographic* magazine (published monthly) provides fascinating accounts of peoples and places around the world—with great photography. Look for issues at the library or start your own collection (back numbers are a mainstay at many garage sales). To subscribe to *National Geographic*, call 800-NGS-LINE, try the Internet at http://www.nationalgeographic.com, or write to

National Geographic Society, P.O. Box 98199, Washington, D.C. 20090-8199.

❀ Two other good reads for aspiring archaeologists are *Smithsonian* magazine and *Archaeology* magazine. Both are published monthly and should be available at most libraries and major newsstands. Following is subscription information for each of these magazines. For *Archaeology*: call 800-829-5122, find subscription information on the Internet at http://www.archaeology.org, or take the more traditional route and write to P.O. Box 420423, Palm Coast, Florida 32142-0423. For *Smithsonian*: call 800-766-2149, look for information on the Internet at http://www.smithsonianmag.si.edu, or write 900 Jefferson Drive, SW, Room 1301, MRC 406, Washington, D.C. 20560.

❀ If your interest is serious enough, you may want to drop some hints about receiving a subscription to one of these magazines as a birthday, Hanukah, or Christmas gift—grandparents are particularly good at picking up the hints!

HIGH-TECH DIGS

Here are some addresses for fascinating on-line archaeology sites on the World Wide Web.

❀ Links to the Past (http://www.cr.nps.gov) from the National Park Service provides information on archaeological and historical sites within national parks.

❀ Internet Resource Guide for Heritage Conservation, Historic Preservation and Archaeology (http://www.cr. nps.gov/ncptt/irg) is a great way to link up with historic societies and archaeologists.

❀ Andersonville National Historic Site (http://www. nps.gov/ande.htm) lets you learn about the 1989 and 1990 excavations at a Civil War prisoner-of-war camp in Georgia.

❀ The Jamestown Rediscovery Project (http://www. widomaker.com/~apva) details findings at the first permanent English settlement in the New World, built in 1607.

☀ National Geographic Online (http://www.nationalgeo-graphic.com) entertaining, virtual-reality walk-throughs of various sites.

TIME CAPSULE

Do your part for the archaeologists of the future. Prepare a time capsule and bury it in your backyard for archaeologists to find in some distant century. Think about the kinds of objects that would provide the most telling evidence about our society, wrap each item in current newspapers, and place them in an airtight container (beg one of those plastic containers from the kitchen) and dig away. Make sure you get permission before you dig!

If a century or two seems too long to wait, make a date to dig it up yourself after some momentous occasion—graduation from college, the birth of your first child (yikes!), or whatever.

HAVE SHOVEL, WILL TRAVEL

If you've really caught the archaeology bug, you won't be content to just read about all these discoveries for long. Eventually, you'll want to see things for yourself. Opportunities abound for forays into the past.

First, find out what's happening in your own backyard (or at least nearby). Three sources of local information include

☀ Your local chapter of the Archaeological Institute of America (write to address listed below for a list).

☀ Your state's historic preservation office. Every state has one. Check the phone book for the office in your state.

☀ Natural History or Living History museums in your area. Be sure to ask the curator or tour guide for tips on other exhibits or projects in the area. You never know until you ask!

☀ Call the Passport in Time Clearinghouse at 800-281-9176 to get information about archaeological and historic

preservation projects sponsored by the U.S. Forest Service. These projects are supervised by professional archaeologists but open for public participation. Make sure to ask them to add your name to their mailing list—they send out a newsletter twice a year that is full of information about interesting projects.

Keep digging—there is lots of exciting work being done in this field.

CHECK IT OUT

Below are listed the two main sources of information about archaeology.

Archaeological Institute of America
656 Beacon Street
Boston, Massachusetts 02215-2010
Students can join this professional group for a minimal fee. It's a great source of information and contacts.

Society for American Archaeology
900 Second Street NE, Suite 12
Washington, D.C. 20002-3557

These organizations that follow offer noteworthy programs.

Crow Canyon Archaeological Center
23390 County Road K
Cortez, Colorado 81321
800-422-8975

EARTHWATCH
680 Mt. Auburn Street
Box 9104
Watertown, Massachusetts 02272

Smithsonian Institution
Research Expedition Program
490 L'Enfant Plaza, Suite 4210
Washington, D.C. 20560

GET ACQUAINTED

Carol J. Ellick, Archaeologist

CAREER PATH

CHILDHOOD ASPIRATION: To be an artist, because everyone told her she was good at drawing.

FIRST JOB: Picking through people's garbage (really!) as part of The Garbage Project at University of Arizona. Gross as it sounds, it was part of an anthropological study about modern day life.

CURRENT JOB: Coordinator of public education and public outreach at Statistical Research Inc., a cultural resource management firm.

Carol J. Ellick brings archaeology to the classroom.

THE DEFINING MOMENT

Carol Ellick was lucky. She knew what she wanted and she knew how to get it. Well, sort of. Actually, she's had the pluck and imagination to link a string of seemingly unrelated interests and occurrences into a fascinating archaeological career spanning over 20 years.

When she was 14 years old, her family took a cross-country trip to Mesa Verde in Colorado to see the cliff dwellings. While there, they visited a little museum. Things clicked for her when she saw a big pot lying on its side with kernels of corn falling out of it. The realization that this scene was reconstructed from the home of a person who lived over 800 years ago was mind-boggling. It added the human factor to the archaeological process and, although she didn't realize it at the time, this was a turning point in her life.

ONE THING LEADS TO ANOTHER

She studied and dug and studied some more until she received a degree in anthropology with an emphasis in archaeology. After graduating, she spent the summer fighting fires with the Forest Service in Oregon—the hardest work she's ever done in her life, she says. Although this particular job had nothing to do with her chosen vocation, it led to a big break in archaeology. While she was working there she met the Forest Service's district archaeologist and talked to him about the field. One thing lead to another. . . .

WHAT GOES AROUND, COMES AROUND

The Forest Service archaeologist asked her if she could draw some pictures of artifacts that they had found. Could she draw? Of course she could draw. She had been drawing great sketches of people and objects since she was a child. She had always wanted to be an artist. Ellick drew the sketches, was offered a job as a scientific illustrator, and a career was born. Almost as a fluke, Ellick was able to combine her two great talents and interests in life—art and archaeology—as a career.

AND THAT'S NOT ALL

Illustrating was also how she found her current job. After obtaining a master's degree in education, her present boss offered her a position coordinating the firm's public education projects. Whether it's designing a brochure about an excavation site, creating a display for schools or museums, conducting site tours, or training teachers how to make archaeology come alive to their students, Ellick continues to perfect her niche as an archaeological artist.

ADVICE TO YOUNG ARCHAEOLOGISTS

Ellick has a young daughter of her own. She encourages her daughter to explore what she wants, to learn from experiences, and to make her own path. Good advice for you, too!

Astronomer

WHAT IS AN ASTRONOMER?

Here's a riddle for you. Why is the oldest science also the youngest science? Astronomy is often considered the oldest science because it represents one of the earliest scientific activities of humankind. Since the beginning of recorded history, people have been looking to the stars for answers about the universe. Yet, it's also the youngest because year after year new discoveries are made that change ideas about the nature of the universe.

Astronomers use the principles of physics and mathematics to study the universe—

the Sun, Moon, planets, stars, and galaxies. They study objects millions and even billions of light-years away. Since you can't put a star in a test tube, they use complex computers and telescopes to do their work. Contrary to what you might expect, few astronomers spend more than a few days or nights per year working at a telescope. More time is spent at the computer—analyzing and interpreting data and writing research reports.

Astronomy is one profession you can't fake your way through. Either you love it with an all-consuming passion or you shouldn't be in the field. The combination of a quality education, ability, and genuine interest in the subject make it easier to find a job in a profession where there are often more job-seekers than jobs. Fortunately, the strenuous training involved in preparing for a career in astronomy also provides an excellent background for other fields such as optics, computer science, physics, and engineering.

The American Astronomical Society advises that "decisions made in high school can have a big effect on a science career. Students who take science and math courses after the tenth grade have the best chance of successfully pursuing a science or engineering career." Make sure precalculus, chemistry, and physics appear on your class schedule before you graduate.

Most astronomers work at universities or colleges where they often combine teaching and research responsibilities. About a third of astronomers work at national observatories or government laboratories such as NASA, the Naval Research Laboratory, the U.S. Naval Observatory, the National Radio Astronomy Observatory, the National Optical Astronomy Observatories, and the Space Telescope Science Institute. A smaller percentage work in business or the aerospace industry. Astronomers can also be found working in planetariums, science museums, secondary schools, or in the science journalism field.

Astronomers see the universe as a gigantic puzzle and try to put each piece together. How are your puzzle-working skills? Ready for the ultimate challenge?

TRY IT OUT
SCIENCE FACT OR FICTION?

Following are astronomical discoveries made in the past two decades. Find out all you can about them at the library and on the Internet. Record your discoveries in a notebook designated just for science observation projects.

black holes	"great walls" of galaxies
brown dwarfs	light echoes around exploding stars
cosmic jets	pulsars
Einstein rings	quasars
gamma ray bursters	voids in space
gravitational lenses	

GALAXY DETECTIVE

Interplanetary spacecraft have observed in explicit detail eight of the nine planets in the Sun's orbit. Find out which eight these are, and record details about each planet in your science observation notebook.

Why haven't spacecraft been able to observe the ninth planet? Make a plan for overcoming this obstacle by the year 2020.

THE MUST-HAVE RESOURCES

If astronomy is in your future, you'd better start getting acquainted with some of those glittery stars. There are some really cool astronomy gizmos on the market that can make this as fun as it is instructive. Check out the best educational products store near you or order some of the following materials.

⚛ A basic astronomy kit called Galaxy Guide is put out by Educational Insights. This comes with everything you need to identify and locate constellations, stars, and planets in the night sky. Look for it in an educational toy

store or order it directly from the company at 16941 Keegan Avenue, Carson, California 90746.

☼ The makers of the SimCity products have come up with a CD for astronomy enthusiasts. Red Shift 2 lets you explore the universe via virtual reality simulations, super-realistic models, solar hitchhiking, and animated tours. It is available from Maxis Multimedia Ltd. at 2121 North California Boulevard, Walnut Creek, California 94596-3572. The phone number is 800-33-MAXIS

☼ ROM Tech, Inc. produces several awesome-sounding space interest products including Distant Suns: An Interactive Space and Solar System Explorer—it's like having a full-fledged planetarium on your computer screen. The company's address is 2945 McMillan Avenue, Suite 128, San Luis Obispo, California 93401.

☼ The program Guide: CD-ROM Star Chart, Version 2.0, is recommended for both those new to the sky and those with years of experience in astronomy. It includes things like the Hubble Guide Star Catalog—showing the positions for and magnitudes of about 15 million stars. It should keep you busy for a while. It can be ordered from Project Pluto, Ridge Road Box 1607, Bowdoinham, Maine 04008.

REV UP THE SEARCH ENGINE

Internet search engines are getting easier and more effective to use. To use most search engines all you have to do is type the word or phrase that describes what you are looking for. In a matter of seconds you'll have access to information from all over the world. For space-related information, simply type *astronomy* and have fun exploring all the information your search yields.

There are a couple of sites you won't want to miss, including

☼ The home page for the Space Telescope Science Institute, which includes some amazing pictures, news updates, educational activities, and links to other resources. Find it on the Internet at http://www.stsci.edu.

- Project Astro is a joint project of the National Science Foundation and NASA, and it links students and teachers with astronomers and astronomy happenings around the world. Find out about this project at http://www.asp-sky.org/subpages/proj.html.
- For up-to-the-minute news on space visit a site called Today at NASA at http://www.hq.nasa.gov/office/pao/NewsRoom/today.html.
- For links to the Hubble Space Telescope and other interesting space information go to http://msn.yahoo.com/science/space/satellites/missions/telescopes/Hubble_Space_Telescope.

CHECK IT OUT

American Association of Variable Star Observers
25 Birch Street
Cambridge, Massachusetts 02138

American Astronomical Society
Executive Office
2000 Florida Avenue NW, Suite 400
Washington, D.C. 20009

Astronomical League
Science Service Building
1719 N Street NW
Washington, D.C. 20036
Ask about local amateur astronomy clubs! There are thousands of them around the country!

Center for Advanced Space Studies
Lunar and Planetary Institute
3600 Bay Area Boulevard
Houston, Texas 77058-1113

National Space Science Data Center
NASA Goddard Space Flight Center
Mail Code 933.4
Greenbelt, Maryland 20771

GET ACQUAINTED

Professor Gibor Basri,
Astronomer

CAREER PATH

CHILDHOOD ASPIRATION:
Ever since he was six years old working in astronomy was his goal. In eighth grade he did a career report and found out that astronomy wasn't a great choice because it's a small field. He started out studying physics in college but decided to "go for it" in graduate school.

FIRST JOB: Washing dishes in his college dormitory. He only lasted two weeks because he discovered too many inefficiencies, corrected them, and worked himself out of a pay-by-the-hour job.

CURRENT JOB: Professor of astronomy at the University of California teaching everything from introductory freshmen courses to very technical graduate seminars.

MOST EXCITING DISCOVERY (SO FAR)

Brown dwarfs are a celestial object somewhere between a planet and a star in size and brightness, and Basri announced the first brown dwarf ever to be authenticated in June 1995. Others have been discovered since then. Basri's discovery was made possible because of access to the University of California's Keck telescope—the world's largest telescope.

It took a while to get it right. The first test failed, and he had to backtrack to figure out why. It eventually became apparent that the star cluster containing the brown dwarf was older—and therefore fainter—than he had originally thought. His hard work and perseverance paid off in the end.

PUBLISH OR PERISH

With 60 major research papers to his credit, Basri is in no danger of "perishing" in the academic world. Among his titles are *Lithium and Brown Dwarf Candidates: The Mass and Age of the Faintest Pleiades Stars*, *A Surprise at the Bottom of the Main Sequence: Rapid Rotation and No Alpha Emission*, and *Limits on the Magnetic Flux on Pre-Main Sequence Stars*. You won't find these works at your local bookstore, but they represent important contributions to the study of the universe.

IS THERE LIFE ON OTHER PLANETS?

Basri says yes, bacterial life at the very least. And, with so many planets and galaxies left unexplored, who knows? maybe there really is such a thing as ETs. Expect someone (maybe you'll be the one) to discover life on another planet (possibly even life similar to what we know on Earth) in your lifetime.

BEST ADVICE FOR POTENTIAL ASTRONOMERS

Get on it early! Start taking as many science and math courses as you can beginning in junior high. It's easier to move out of science into other fields than it is to move into science from other fields. If you haven't established a good background in math and science by the end of high school, you're in trouble.

Chemist

SKILL SET

✔ COMPUTERS

✔ SCIENCE

✔ MATH

WHAT IS A CHEMIST?

What does your body have in common with a compact disc, a book, a hockey puck, and a can of paint? They're all made out of chemicals. Chemists are the people who put chemicals together in various ways to create new products or solve specific problems.

Many chemists work in laboratories equipped with state-of-the-art (awesome) equipment. Their work can involve everything from developing everyday products like deodorant and makeup to looking for cures to diseases like AIDS. They also work to preserve and improve our food, air, and water.

Almost half of chemists work as researchers exploring new processes and developing or improving products. Following are descriptions of some chemistry specialties:

Agricultural chemists develop and test the chemicals used to aid crop production—herbicides, fungicides, and insecticides.

Environmental chemists look at how to protect our world from contaminants and pollution problems.

Materials scientists integrate applications from many scientific disciplines to develop products such as metals, ceramics, rubber, and paint.

Pharmaceutical chemists develop medicines using natural ingredients from plants and synthetic drug compounds.

Polymer chemists apply specialized technology to a variety of applications including plastics, adhesives, and biomedical products such as artificial skin and nicotine patches.

College is a must for anyone pursuing a career in this field. A two-year associate of arts degree prepares you for work as a chemical technician. Further education provides more advanced opportunities. The most successful chemists carefully blend a broad knowledge of the sciences with a highly focused specialty. As with any scientific endeavor, chemists must learn how to learn and to be adaptable to new technology and frequent advances in the field.

TRY IT OUT

MIX IT UP

Become a kitchen chemist! There are several ways to find "recipes" for experiments:

☼ Go to the library and look for books with ideas—there are many books that include chemistry experiments. Ask the librarian to help you find some good ones. Especially

35

look for anything by Janice Van Cleave—she knows how to make it fun!

- 💡 Get a chemistry kit from your local educational toy store. At a good store, you'll find everything from the basics to some fairly sophisticated kits. Buy one that fits your budget and level of expertise.
- 💡 Check out Internet resources. One recent cruise down the information highway netted 40,205 matches for *kitchen chemistry*. That's enough to keep even the most avid chemistry fan busy for a while.

Remember to follow all instructions and be extremely careful. Some chemicals simply don't mix well with others. Be sure you know which ones are which BEFORE you mix them.

COMPUTER CHEMISTRY

The Internet comes through as an outstanding source of information for aspiring chemists. The following sites are full of information and links to an incredible array of chemistry resources.

- 💡 The Internet Chemistry Resource is an award-winning site and can be found at http://www.rpi.edu/dept/chem/cheminfo/chemres.html.
- 💡 The Chemware Home Page includes educational materials and activities, as well as software to order and shareware that you can download on your computer for free. The site is located at http://users.iconz.co.nz/trout/default.html.
- 💡 Stay a step ahead of the game with a visit to a site frequented by chemistry teachers. You'll find experiments, demonstrations and other activities at http://home.fuse.net/thecatalyst/.
- 💡 An absolute must for young chemists is The Chemistry Place. The Web address is http://chemplace.com. After a trial membership there is a minimal fee to belong. The cost is well worth it because this site is jam-packed with learning activities, weekly chemistry riddles, research news, and more.

PROJECT SEED

The American Chemical Society sponsors a summer program that gives high school students from economically disadvantaged homes the opportunity to experience science research in a laboratory work environment. Ask your parent or science teacher to call 202-872-4380 to see if any Project SEED programs are available in your area.

CHECK IT OUT

American Association of Pharmaceutical Scientists
601 King Street
Alexandria, Virginia 22314-3105

American Chemical Society
Education Division
1155 16th Street NW
Washington, D.C. 20036
This group produces some outstanding career-related materials. Find out about the society's magazine for high school chemistry students called *Chem Matters*. It also sponsors a program called the National Chemistry Olympiad. Write them to find out about activities in your area.

American Institute of Chemical Engineering
345 East 47th Street
New York, New York 10017-2395
800-242-4363

Chemical Specialties Manufacturers Association
1001 Connecticut Avenue NW
Washington, D.C. 20036

National Agricultural Chemicals Association
1155 15th Street NW, Suite 900
Washington, D.C. 20005

Society of Plastics Engineers
14 Fairfield Drive
Brookfield, Connecticut 06804

GET ACQUAINTED
Ellen Molner, Perfumer

CAREER PATH

CHILDHOOD ASPIRATION:
To be a "mommy" and a professional.

FIRST JOB: Lab technician
for a perfume company.

CURRENT JOB: Perfumer.

HAVE DEGREE, WILL WORK

Molner graduated from college with a degree in biology only to find that biology jobs were few and far between. With her unusual mix of artsiness and scientific knowledge to her approach, she wasn't sure which way to go with her career.

As fate would have it, answering a help-wanted ad sealed her destiny. The ad read simply "seeking lab tech, high school o.k., college even better." She ended up assisting a chief per-fumer—making compounds of the perfumer's formula—and discovered a whole new world of "creative" science.

The perfumer she worked for soon noticed her talent and offered her the opportunity to apprentice under him.

THE NOSE KNOWS

Her first task as a perfumer was to "develop a nose"—trade talk for learning to identify some 3,000 to 4,000 raw materials with a sniff. You've either got it or you don't when it comes to an olfactory skill like this. Luckily, Molner had it and was on her way to a fascinating career in this unusual specialty.

As daunting as this initial process sounds, Molner says that after 20 years in the business she is so familiar with various scents that she can smell them in her sleep!

A PERFUME IS BORN

It starts with an idea. Clients come with a profile of a product they would like to bring to market. The profile contains all kinds of demographic information about the intended user: how old they are, how much money they make, what kinds of food they like to eat, their education level, what they want to smell like, etc. Perfumers keep these personal preferences in mind to develop scents that appeal to a specific audience.

Trends in society also dictate the way perfumes are designed. For instance, fragrances in the 1980s tended to be "loud" and ostentatious, and they were made with complicated mixes. Fragrances for the 1990s reflected simple, yet sophisticated tastes with subtle differences between products for males and females.

Social scientist is just one more hat that perfumers wear to make sure that their potions meet with consumer demand.

YOU WIN SOME AND YOU LOSE SOME

Molner describes her work as 99 percent perspiration and 1 percent satisfaction. It's a tough, competitive business, and you don't always win the job. It's a real thrill to walk into a store and see a product that you had a hand in developing.

THANK HEAVENS FOR COMPUTERS

Computers store ingredient lists and information used to check chemical combinations for toxicology and safety standards (there isn't much demand for combustible or poisonous cologne!). This technology makes the work of a perfumer much easier.

ADVICE FOR YOUNG CHEMISTS

Molner heartily endorses a career in chemistry and says that there is always a need for serious scientists who can develop new chemistry. While jobs in the perfume industry are limited, there is plenty of room for chemists who can combine scientific process and creativity.

Engineer

WHAT IS AN ENGINEER?

Airplanes, oil fields, coal mines, automobile factories, skyscrapers—these are just a few of the places where you might find an engineer. Engineers are problem-solvers. They use the laws of math and science to figure out practical solutions to problems in many types of industries. Their job is to think up ways to use power and materials to make our world a better, safer, and more efficient place.

The oldest and most commonly known type of engineer is the civil engineer. These engineers design and guide the construction of structures such as buildings, roads, tunnels, bridges, and water systems. They also help reduce air pollution, improve transportation systems, and purify drinking water.

Other types of engineering specialists include the following:

Aerospace engineers work with aircraft, missiles and spacecraft.

Chemical engineers make new and better products from chemicals like rubber and petroleum. They create products like detergents, medicines, and plastics.

Electrical engineers harness electrical energy to operate things such as automobiles, computers, televisions, and missile guidance systems.

Industrial engineers work with people, machines, energy, and materials to figure out the best way to do a certain task. Their job is to find ways to get more out of less.

Manufacturing engineers start with 200 basic manufacturing processes and more than 40,000 materials to develop new processes for making products that range in sophistication from a jet fighter to a tube of lipstick.

Mechanical engineers work on two kinds of machines—either those that produce power like rocket engines or machines that use power like refrigerators.

Metallurgical engineers work to develop methods to process and convert metals into usable forms.

Mining engineers find, extract, and prepare minerals such as coal and copper for manufacturing use.

Nuclear engineers conduct research on the use of nuclear energy and radiation to generate electricity or for medical purposes.

Petroleum engineers explore and drill for oil and gas.

And still other specialties include

automotive engineering

agricultural engineering

architectural engineering

ceramic engineering

computer engineering

environmental engineering

fire protection engineering

geological engineering

geothermal engineering

heating, ventilation, and
refrigeration engineering

materials engineering

naval engineering

ocean engineering

plastics engineering

robotics and automated
systems engineering

safety engineering

software engineering

transportation
engineering

Needless to say with a list that long, engineering is a big field full of exciting opportunities. It's a demanding field but very rewarding both in terms of income potential and job satisfaction. Engineers are in demand in industry, business, government, research, teaching, and the military.

Most engineering jobs require at least a bachelor's degree, and many engineers go on to obtain a master's degree while they are working. Another way into the field is as an engineering technician, which requires only a degree from a two-year program.

So, what are you going to do when you grow up? How does designing a system to colonize the moon grab you? What about developing new laser technology that will save lives? And there's always the possibility of developing clean, efficient fuels out of garbage. Whatever you do as an engineer, you are sure to be on the cutting edge of technology and will help shape the next century.

TRY IT OUT

HIT THE BOOKS

Go to the library and ask the librarian to help you find books about the particular type of engineering that you are most interested in. While you are there, see what kinds of information you can find about some of the most spectacular engineering feats that the world has ever seen: the Panama Canal, the Golden Gate Bridge, and shuttle spacecraft.

The two books below are full of challenging projects for the budding engineer. Check them out of your local library. If your library doesn't have a copy, ask your librarian to order one.

Goodwin, Robert H. *Engineering Projects for Young Scientists.* New York: Franklin Watts, 1987.

Wood, Robert W. *Science for Kids: 39 Easy Engineering Experiments.* Blue Ridge Summit, Penn.: TAB Books, 1992.

WANDER ALONG THE INFORMATION HIGHWAY

Use your computer to connect with engineering forums on the World Wide Web. Engineers from all over the world chat about current problems and issues via computer modem. If you don't have access to the Internet on your computer at home, try your school or public library. Many public libraries have access to these types of programs.

Use an Internet search engine to help you find information about a specific area you are interested in. For example, type in *aerospace engineering* and get ready to blast off!

PUT YOUR SKILLS TO THE TEST

Compete in science fairs like the Science Olympiad. To get information about contests in your area, write 5955 Little Pine Lane, Rochester, Minnesota 48064.

Another great way to stretch your skills is with the Odyssey of the Mind (OM) program. OM provides opportunities for kids to develop divergent thinking and creative problem-solving skills (important for all types of engineers) while working with others on team projects. For information about OM programs in your area, contact Odyssey of the Mind, P.O. Box 547, Glassboro, New Jersey 08028-0547.

The National Society of Professional Engineers sponsors MATHCOUNTS competitions across the country as a way to increase awareness of math-related career opportunities. Call the MATHCOUNTS hotline at 703-684-2828 for more information or e-mail to mathcounts@nspe.org.

If engineering is even a remote possibility for your future, you need to find out about JETS (Junior Engineering Technical Society). This group has an awesome array of programs and materials designed to help you make an informed decision. Top on the list is TEAMS (Tests of Engineering Aptitude, Mathematics and Science), an academic program and team competition to teach high schoolers team development and problem-solving skills. Write to the address listed in Check It Out or visit them out on the Internet at jets@nas.edu.

Find out if your local college, university, or natural history museum offers summer science or math camps. These can be great opportunities to apply your knowledge from reading to challenging experiments and projects.

CD-ROMS YOU GOTTA TRY

☼ SimCity 2000 and all its various add-ons (the Urban Renewal kit is a good one for budding engineers) offer a great combination of the challenging with the entertaining. You can find these programs at most software stores or order directly from the publisher by calling 800-33-MAXIS.

☼ The Way Things Work 2.0 is another fun choice. It features 150 machines and gives the scientific principles

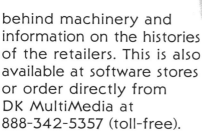

behind machinery and information on the histories of the retailers. This is also available at software stores or order directly from DK MultiMedia at 888-342-5357 (toll-free).

CHECK IT OUT

American Society for
  Engineering Education
11 Dupont Circle, Suite 200
Washington, D.C. 20036

Junior Engineering Technical
  Society (JETS)
1420 King Street, Suite 405
Alexandria, Virginia 22314

Society of Women Engineers
345 East 47th Street, Suite 305
New York, New York 10017

GET ACQUAINTED

Rose Lindsey,
Industrial Engineer

CAREER PATH

CHILDHOOD ASPIRATION: Wasn't sure but noticed that she really liked math classes—especially solving problems, getting the answer "X = ," and underlining it twice!

NASA engineer Rose Lindsey (left) tours a replica of the space shuttle with author Diane Reeves and Reeves's daughters.

FIRST JOB: Industrial engineer at the Charleston Naval Supply Yard in Charleston, South Carolina.

CURRENT JOB: NASA payload operations director (POD) at NASA's Marshall Space Flight Center in Huntsville, Alabama.

As POD, Rose Lindsey leads a payload operations control center (POCC) cadre, or group, of 15 to 20 people who support scientists and engineers from around the world when they conduct payload operations (experiments) onboard the shuttle spacelab missions.

The POCC cadre is responsible for sending instructions to astronauts conducting spacelab experiments. These instructions may be verbal or telescience commands from the ground to adjust experiment operations.

MOST EXCITING PROJECTS

Several projects top Lindsey's list of favorites: The First International Microgravity (IML-1), the Second Astronomy Mission (ASTRO-II), the United States Microgravity Payloads (USMP-1, USMP-2, USMP-3), and the Tethered Satellite System Reflight Mission (TSS-1R) are just a few of the NASA missions with which Lindsey has been involved.

She says one of the best parts of her job is working with so many interesting scientists from many parts of the world including Canada, Europe, and Russia.

BIGGEST SURPRISE ON THE JOB

Even though Lindsey's technical background in engineering is vital to her work with scientists and astronauts, Lindsey was surprised to learn that her writing and speaking skills were just as important. Working with so many different types of people from diverse cultures poses a continual challenge to Lindsey's communication and diplomatic abilities!

LINDSEY'S ADVICE TO FUTURE ENGINEERS

Find something that you love to do and a place where you can contribute something you believe in. Gain a solid engineering background that you can build on. Also, take advantage of any summer internships or cooperative education programs your school sponsors to get a firsthand look at engineering careers.

Food Scientist

SHORTCUTS

GO carry out a French fry taste test. Visit as many fast-food restaurants as you can and find out which one makes the best fries.

READ the back of cereal boxes and other processed food to find out what things are made from.

TRY creating your own recipe. Start with some chocolate chip cookie dough, add a little imagination, and see what you come up with.

SKILL SET

✔ BUSINESS

✔ MATH

✔ SCIENCE

WHAT IS A FOOD SCIENTIST?

As long as people need to eat, there will be opportunities in the food industry. If you've ever seen how much food a middle school football team can consume in one meal, it won't surprise you to learn that food is the world's largest industry. Billions of people depend on food scientists to find ways to feed the world efficiently and economically. With worldwide goals, it's no wonder that the field of food science is ripe with opportunity. So ripe, in fact, that the U.S. Bureau of Labor Statistics projects a 20 to 30 percent increase in jobs in that area by the year 2005.

Food scientists use chemistry, microbiology, engineering, and other basic and applied sciences to find ways to produce, process, present, evaluate, and distribute food. Their work can be as diverse as managing a food firm, conducting research to improve flavor and shelf life, inspecting foods as part of a quality control process, or designing new packaging techniques. Food scientists are behind developments such as juice-in-a-box, fun fruits, and all those new-fangled foods you find at fast-food restaurants.

Following are quick descriptions of some of the main specialties of this field:

Food processing involves converting raw foods into beverages, cereals, dairy products, meat and seafood products, fruit and vegetable products, snacks and convenience foods, and foods for animals.

Food research often means working in labs, test kitchens, and on production lines. Food researchers look for ways to improve the nutritional value, purity, taste, appearance, shelf life, convenience, and safety of foods while reducing their cost. They also work on developing new foods and finding solutions to the world's food problems.

Food biotechnology is a cutting-edge area. In a quest to improve crop production and quality and to produce raw products that can be converted into nutritious foods, some food scientists work with the highly specialized processes of plant breeding, gene splicing, microbial fermentation, and tissue cultures.

Food manufacturing involves building brand new foods from unusual sources.

Variety, opportunity, challenge: The field of food science has them waiting for a new generation of scientists. Think about these few food science problems waiting for you to solve:

☼ finding ways to turn low-cost food sources like soybeans, grains, and fishmeal into edible munchies
☼ developing foods for the first moon colony
☼ making broccoli and brussels sprouts as appealing to children as candy bars are
☼ improving methods for harvesting foods to expand the world's food supply
☼ inventing cool new snack foods for the kids of tomorrow

TRY IT OUT

GO TO CYBER SCHOOL

Learn all you need to know to decide if a future in food science is the right choice for you. Do this by taking a complete minicourse on the food industry—compliments of the World Wide Web.

Introduction to the Food Industry is a self-study learning tool designed to help students explore the food industry and its career opportunities. You can link up to this self-taught and self-paced course at http://www.ift.org/car/food_ind/intro.html.

Eight interesting and interactive lessons will guide you through food safety and quality assurance, food processing (how do you make peanut butter anyway?), nutrition, labeling and packaging, integrated resource management (huh?), distributing food from plant to store, marketing foods to shoppers, providing customer service, and preparing foods at home. Its lessons include learning objectives, a subject overview, career information, activities, questions, and lists of additional resources.

If you have even a teeny, tiny interest in this field, check out this Institute of Food Technologists website!

THE CORN CONNECTION

Corn: It's yellow. It's crunchy. It's fun to eat straight off the cob. Yeah, so what?

It's also an ingredient in many of the foods you eat. Go through the kitchen cupboards, read the food labels and make a list of all the foods that contain some form of corn (starch, syrup, meal, etc.).

Next go to the library and find out all you can about how to process corn and why it's used in so many foods.

If you really get into your research, try the same process finding all the different food additives listed as ingredients in the food in your cabinets.

PLAY WITH YOUR FOOD

The Institute of Food Technologists will send you a 32-page booklet with instructions for eight fairly easy food experiments. Request a copy from the address listed in Check It Out and have fun learning about the scientific principles of food.

CHECK IT OUT

American Council on Science and Health
1995 Broadway, Second Floor
New York, New York 10023-5860

Center for Nutrition Policy and Information
1120 20th Street NW
Suite 200, North Lobby
Washington, D.C. 20036

Institute of Food Technologists
221 North LaSalle Street
Chicago, Illinois 60601
Ask for a copy of the brochure *World's Largest Food Industry*. It describes a variety of opportunities in food science and technology.

National Agricultural Library
Food and Nutrition Information Center
10301 Baltimore Avenue, Room 304
Beltsville, Maryland 20705-2351
Check them out on the Internet too: http://www.nal.usda.gov/fnic.

Society for Nutrition Education
2001 Killebrew Drive, Suite 340
Minneapolis, Minnesota 55425-1882

GET ACQUAINTED

Greg Socha,
Food Scientist

CAREER PATH

CHILDHOOD ASPIRATION: To be a professional baseball player.

FIRST JOB: Started helping out on his family's farm when he was five years old.

CURRENT JOB: Director of new product development for Boston Market restaurants.

As long as people eat fast food Greg Socha will have a job. And, as long as Socha is on the job, people will eat well. He is part of a research and development team that dreams up new ideas for food products sold in a chain of upscale fast-food restaurants. Recent creations include desserts, pasta salads, a new Caesar salad, and a scrumptious holiday sweet potato dish.

IT'S MORE THAN SECRET INGREDIENTS

Of course, Socha has to know a lot about food. But, he has to know a lot about people and business, too. He has to know what people crave, the latest trends, and how much people will pay for food. He also has to understand the business of food—what the competition is up to, what his vendors can make, and how to get his great ideas to the marketplace.

Socha's work involves researching food and market trends (he has to eat out a lot, poor guy), testing new ideas in the lab, talking with customers about their likes and dislikes, and tracking the progress of several products through an intensive development process. It usually only takes a few months to develop and launch a new product, so he really has to keep things rolling.

Because the industry is so broad and diverse, Socha recommends that food scientists learn a little about a whole lot of things. That's called being a generalist—following this advice will prepare you to tackle all kinds of job situations.

IT STARTED BACK IN MOM'S KITCHEN

Socha says he's always been around food. He grew up on a dairy farm and got a birds-eye view of the beginning of the food process. His mother was a great cook and taught him how to find his way around the kitchen. He helped with canning, making wedding cakes, and family meals. When he got a little older, he did his farm chores in the morning, went to school during the day, and worked the evening shift in a restaurant.

All this gave him a great perspective about the end of the food process. But it also made him curious about what happens in the middle. He went to college at the University of Georgia to find out.

After graduating, Socha got his start as a food scientist developing new products with Pizza Hut. He was part of a team that created the hand-tossed traditional pizza. He also helped develop the concept of making pizzas available in high pedestrian areas like colleges and airports. If your school sells pizza for lunch, you have Socha to thank.

Later, at Burger King, Socha helped introduce a new concept called "co-branding," in which two or more businesses share space at a single location. For instance, the restaurant might team up with a gas station and mini-grocery store. It's a smart idea that helps cut costs and get branded foods to places that wouldn't otherwise have them.

THE GUMBY THEORY APPLIES

Work in research and development requires a lot of flexibility. What's hot at one minute can be out the next, and something that was out six months ago may be hot today. Socha calls it "the Gumby theory," and he has to be ready to go with the flow.

A MENU OF OPPORTUNITY

Everyone in the world needs to eat, so there's bound to be plenty of opportunity in this field for a long time to come. Socha heartily recommends it to those who have a passion for food and an interest in business.

Horticulturist

SHORTCUTS

GO take a hike, camp out overnight—anything that gets you outdoors, surrounded by nature.

READ *Farmer's Almanac* for some down-to-earth insight into growing things.

TRY growing plants from seeds—in a garden, homemade greenhouse, or window box.

WHAT IS A HORTICULTURIST?

Horticulture is an applied plant science. It combines art and science in the production, marketing, use, and improvement of fruits, vegetables, flowers, and ornamental plants. Horticulture is often a hobby (sometimes closer to an addiction) that's practiced in backyard gardens everywhere. People that actually make their living in horticulture are the envy of millions of amateur gardeners around the world.

Some of the ways that horticulturists practice the profession are

- maintaining botanical gardens, arboretums, and public parks
- owning and/or operating a wholesale or retail source of flowers, fruit, vegetables, or plants (for example, a garden center, nursery, greenhouse, farmer's market, or flower shop)
- teaching at colleges and universities or working in cooperative extension programs
- providing consultation services in landscaping, pest management, and other horticultural disciplines
- conducting research and development activities for business in areas like plant breeding, biotechnology, tissue culture, and horticulture chemical product development
- applying the science of raising plants to the business of running a farm to help farmers make a profit (country

agricultural extension offices, research foundations, private farms and nurseries, and seed companies are likely employers)

☀ working for government agencies as plant inspectors, lobbyists, urban tree specialists, and zoning inspectors

☀ serving internationally to help developing countries resolve agricultural problems through programs such as the Peace Corps

Ecological concerns have created more opportunities for horticulturists with an environmentalist's point of view. Called environmental horticulturists, these scientists develop environmentally friendly or "healthy agriculture" techniques. Finding ways to protect crops without using toxic chemicals (pesticides and herbicides) is a major goal of their work. Environmental horticulturists are most often employed by universities or by the U.S. Department of Agriculture (USDA).

Another interesting specialty is horticultural therapy, which involves using plants and horticultural activities to help people who are disabled or disadvantaged. Horticultural therapy is practiced in almost 300 hospitals in the United States, and more than a dozen colleges and universities offer horticultural therapy training programs.

Horticulture is one of those rare (and for many people, wonderful) occupations that combine a way to make a living with a way of life. It's a career that can grow on you if you find the idea of teaming up with Mother Nature appealing.

TRY IT OUT

GROW ON-LINE

You can find an incredible amount of useful informatio about horticulture on-line. Your first stop might be Ohio Sta University's Horticulture in Virtual Perspective (http://ww hcs.ohio-state.edu/hcs/hcs.html). This site includes horticu ture teaching resources—with complete on-line courses o subjects such as:

- ☼ biology of horticulture
- ☼ technology of horticulture
- ☼ history of horticulture
- ☼ plants and horticulture (complete with high resolution pictures)

You'll also find a plant dictionary with more than 1,40 links and descriptions for plants representing 60 types annuals, bulbs, grasses, groundcovers, perennials, shrut trees, and vines. If all that isn't enough, there is also WebGarden Factsheet database with over 5,000 horticultu al factsheets.

One stop for super-snoopers (you'll have to hunt a little f the good stuff) is the USDA National Agricultural Librar (http://www.nal.usda.gov). There you'll find everything fro general information to specific studies on topics as narrow the genetics and breeding of cucurbit species (that's "hor talk for cucumbers, melons, squash, pumpkins, and assorte other relatives).

WHO TURNED OUT THE LIGHTS?

Science quiz! What is photosynthesis?

A. Those little booths in the mall where you can get you picture taken for a dollar.
B. The process through which plants capture light and co vert it to chemical energy (plant food).
C. A fancy name for a one-hour photo developing shop.

Put a smiley face on your paper if you picked B!

Try this simple experiment to see photosynthesis at work. Here's what you'll need:

black construction paper (or use a black marker to completely cover both sides of a white sheet of paper)

1 houseplant
scissors
tape

1. Make two small envelopes with the black paper.
2. Completely cover two leaves with the paper envelopes and secure with tape.
3. Just for fun, cut the remaining black paper into shapes and tape the shapes onto a couple leaves.
4. Put the plant in a sunny spot and make sure you keep it watered as usual.
5. After a week, uncover the leaves.
6. Record the results in a notebook.
7. Consider the following list of questions and see if you can come up with answers:
   ♀ How did the covered leaves respond to the lack of light?
   ♀ What does that tell you about photosynthesis?
   ♀ What happened to the leaves covered with the shapes?
   ♀ How are the covered portions different from the uncovered ones?

For more experiments that put your green thumb to the test, check out:

_____

Woods, Robert W. *Science for Kids: 39 Easy Plant Biology Experiments.* Blue Ridge Summit, Penn.: TAB Books, 1991.

_____

GET DOWN AND DIRTY!

There are lots of ways to put your green thumb to the test. Volunteer or apply for part-time jobs at parks, plant nurseries, farms, experiment stations, laboratories, florists, or with landscape architects. Get experience making things grow. Every experienced gardener has a few tricks up their sleeves—ask questions and learn from everyone you meet!

LOOK IT UP

Horticulture is only one of many plant-related careers. If you hope to make a living with your green thumb, you'll want to compare the choices. First, get a notebook. Make headings with the following job titles:

agricultural
  horticulturist
agronomist
arborist
botanist
conservationist
economic botanist

environmental
  horticulturist
forester
mycologist
phytopathologist
plant pathologist
plant taxonomist

Use career encyclopedias and other resources to find out what each occupation involves.

JOIN THE CLUB

The National Junior Horticultural Association (NJHA) offers a variety of programs to help young people learn about and experience horticulture. NJHA provides a menu of projects and activities with participation determined by age, interests, and experience. For information about this program and a list of program leaders in your state, contact NJHA at the address listed in Check It Out.

CHECK IT OUT

American Association of Botanical Gardens and Arboreta
786 Church Road
Wayne, Pennsylvania 19087

American Horticultural Society
7931 East Boulevard Drive
Alexandria, Virginia 22308

American Horticultural Therapy Association
362A Christopher Avenue
Gaithersburg, Maryland 20879

American Phytopathological Society
3340 Pilot Knob Road
St. Paul, Minnesota 55121

American Society for Horticultural Science
600 Cameron Street
Alexandria, Virginia 22314-2562

American Society of Agronomy
677 South Segoe Road
Madison, Wisconsin 53711

American Society of Plant Taxonomists
Department of Botany
University of Wyoming
Laramie, Wyoming 82071-3165

Botanical Society of America
Department of Botany
Ohio State University
11735 Neil Avenue
Columbus, Ohio 43210

Ecological Society of America
2010 Massachusetts Avenue NW, Suite 400
Washington, D.C. 20036

Horticulture Research Institute
1250 I Street NW, Suite 500
Washington, D.C. 20005

Mycological Society of America and Phycological Society of America
P.O. Box 1897
Lawrence, Kansas 66044-8897

National Junior Horticultural Association
401 North Fourth Street
Durant, Oklahoma 74701

Society of American Foresters
5400 Grosvenor Lane
Bethesda, Maryland 20814

GET ACQUAINTED

Julius Nuccio, Horticulturist

IT'S ALL IN THE FAMILY

Julius Nuccio is part of the second generation of family running this California firm started by his father and uncle 62 years ago. The Nuccios specialize in growing camellias and azaleas and are renowned for cultivating some breathtaking varieties. Their flowers are grown outdoors year-round on a 10-acre farm and shipped to buyers all over the world.

CAREER PATH

CHILDHOOD ASPIRATION: Anything but work at his father's nursery.

FIRST JOB: Besides helping with the flowers at the nursery, working in a gas station.

CURRENT JOB: Co-owner of Nuccio Nurseries, growers of world-class camellias and azaleas.

GO TO COLLEGE OR GET TO WORK!

After Nuccio graduated from high school, his father gave him a choice of going to college or getting to work. He didn't like the idea of spending more time in school and had decided that he didn't want to spend the rest of his life pumping gas, so he chose to work at the nursery until he figured out something better to do.

He didn't realize then how much he enjoyed working outdoors, being his own boss, and playing with nature. Now, 40 years later, Nuccio says he has no regrets over his decision.

APPRENTICE TO THE BEST

Unlike many horticulturists, Nuccio has no formal training in the profession. Instead, he learned from the two best teach-

ers in the world—his father and uncle. After years of on-the-job training and a desire to learn something new every day, Nuccio can boast a nursery with the reputation of one of the finest camellia growers in the country.

THE BIRDS AND THE BEES

You'd be amazed to discover how many different kinds of camellias and azaleas there are. That's because horticulturists like Nuccio constantly work to add new specimens to the family by crossbreeding them. By mixing two kinds of flowers, these flower scientists cultivate new species that can differ in color and shape as well as growth habits. For instance, camellias were once only grown in warmer regions of the country. Crossbreeding has resulted in the creation of hardier hybrids that can withstand colder temperatures.

Crossbreeding isn't a quick process. It can take four or five years from the beginning of the process until there is enough stock built up to take to market. While a horticulturist may graft anywhere from 5 to 10,000 seedlings to start the process, it is quite common for only 3 to 10 samples to survive. The cutting and grafting procedure continues until there are enough samples to get a good picture of the new species. A new species is officially born when nature takes over and the birds and the bees start pollinating.

IT GROWS ON YOU

When Nuccio was a teenager, he never expected to be doing what he's doing now and enjoying it so much. Over the years he has found a great deal of satisfaction in his work. He says that horticulture is not a way to get rich quick but that it's a great way to enjoy earning a good living. He encourages anyone with an interest in working with plants to combine learning from books with gaining hands-on experience.

Landscape Architect

SKILL SET

✔ ART

✔ MATH

✔ SCIENCE

GO visit botanical gardens, parks, and other pretty sites.

READ seed catalogs, gardening magazines, and books about nature.

TRY growing things—on the windowsill, in a homemade greenhouse, in a garden.

WHAT IS A LANDSCAPE ARCHITECT?

Close your eyes and imagine your favorite outdoor place. Is it a park? Near the seashore? Your own backyard? Chances are that a landscape architect had a hand in designing some of the beautiful outdoor places you see everyday.

One of the first, and most enduring, examples of landscape architecture in the United States was the design of New York City's Central Park. Two men, Frederick Law Olmsted and Calvert Vaux, combined their talents to create a green oasis of quiet in the middle of a bustling, concrete city.

In simple terms, the goal of a landscape architect is to beautify the places where people live and work. You've seen their handiwork in places like parks, malls, college campuses, corporate sites, cemeteries, resorts, and residential developments. Landscape architects design these areas so that they are functional and compatible with the natural environment.

An emerging specialty within the field is the environmental landscape architect. With an eye toward environmental responsibility and stewardship of the land, environmental landscape architects design, plan, modify, and enhance large tracts of land. Some ecologically conscious projects involve restoring wetlands and woodlands to their natural habitat—sometimes recreating entire ecosystems with the indigenous (native) plants, animals, and birds that once thrived on a particular site. Other projects actually turn garbage dumps into parks.

Another interesting specialty is historic preservation. This work combines a love of history and gardening with design. In order to recreate historically accurate surroundings for historic sites and landmarks, historic preservation landscape architects must dig for details about how people lived and what they grew during a specific time and place in history.

Computers, computer-aided design (CAD) tools, and video simulation equipment are used by all kinds of landscape architects to design livable environments and make detailed plans. They work with teams of urban planners, landscapers, and contractors to implement the plans.

Today's landscape architects must have a strong background in science and be well versed in the areas of ecology, botany, and biology. All this is incorporated into a knowledge of design, construction, plants, and soils. A strenuous testing and licensing process weeds out the unprepared.

Landscape architecture is an appealing profession for those who like to learn on their own, love working outdoors, and don't mind getting their hands dirty.

TRY IT OUT

GET TO KNOW THE LOCAL PLANT LIFE

Find out what flowers and plants are indigenous to your area. Collect and press samples or draw pictures of as many varieties as you can. Make a catalog of your collection and make sure to label everything and include descriptions and instructions for growing them.

DATA UNDER YOUR NAILS

Following are descriptions of some fun gardening software that will give you a chance to design gardens of all colors, shapes, and sizes. Since more products are springing up all the time, you may want to visit a software or office supply store to see the latest.

- ☀ Flowerscape: available for MAC and Windows on floppy discs and CD from Voudette. Call 800-800-1111 to request more information.
- ☀ LandDesigner: available for Windows on CD-ROM only. It is available from Sierra Online at 800-757-7707.
- ☀ 3DLandscape: available for Windows. Call Books That Work at 800-242-4546 for information about this software program.

ENJOY THE SCENERY

Here's the perfect activity for a sunny day while lolling about in a hammock or under a tree; in wintertime substitute for the sunshine a toasty fire in the fireplace or a cozy snuggle under a pile of blankets. Go to the local library and check out a stack of books on landscape architecture. One particularly beautiful and informative volume is *Modern Landscape Architecture: Redefining the Garden* by Felice Frankel and Jory Johnson. It's published by Abbeville Press. Imagine yourself creating these breathtaking scenes. There are many other books. Ask your librarian to help you find them.

BRING YOUR OWN HOE

Link up with your local garden club or botanical garden. These groups can be a great source of education and hands-on learning opportunities. Take classes, go on tours, and volunteer to help with community gardening projects. Listen and learn from people who are madly in love with gardening.

CHECK IT OUT

American Society for Landscape Architects
4401 Connecticut Avenue NW, Fifth Floor
Washington, D.C. 20008-2302
Many states also have local chapters. Find out if there is one near you.

Associated Landscape Contractors of America
12200 Sunrise Valley Drive, Suite 150
Reston, Virginia 22091
A good source for information about alternative opportunities in landscape work.

Society for Ecological Restoration
1207 Seminole Highway, Suite B
Madison, Wisconsin 53711

Environmental Opportunities
Sanford Berry, Editor
P.O. Box 788
Walpole, New Hampshire 02608
Find out about opportunities for landscape architects, urban planners, and backyard gardeners in this publication.

GET ACQUAINTED

Ben Page,
Landscape Architect

CAREER PATH

CHILDHOOD ASPIRATION: To follow the family tradition of medical practice.

FIRST JOB: Working at a Dairy Queen for 90 cents an hour (it was a long time ago).

CURRENT JOB: Owner of a landscape architecture firm.

Ben Page had always planned on becoming a doctor. But, once at college, he discovered that he just wasn't cut out for that profession. His grades starting dropping, and he realized that he needed to come up with another plan fast. He started talking to people whose opinions he respected. One friend encouraged him to think about what he really liked doing.

It didn't take long to figure out that some of his happiest memories centered around his grandparents' farm. He loved being outdoors, was fascinated with design, and was really interested in ecologically based conservation.

Page put aside med school for a new focus: landscape architecture. He transferred to a new school and watched his grades go way up as he found a field of study that fit him better.

FROM THE SIMPLE TO THE EXTRAORDINARY

Page's work as a landscape architect can be as simple as determining the best type of shade tree to use in a client's yard or as complex as a 5-year project restoring a 2,000-acre woodland and animal preserve with natural prairie, marsh, and meadow and an ecologically appropriate food chain. This latter project involved extensive research into things like native grasses, 19th-century plowing techniques, and appropriate food sources for red-tailed hawks.

Page designs beautiful environments for people's homes as well as corporate sites. He has even developed a master plan for the vice president's gardens in Washington, D.C. From now on the vice president will be greeting dignitaries and enjoying private family picnics in style. The formal garden is similar in scale to the Rose Garden at the White House. The private garden is designed to be a relaxing oasis for the nation's "second family."

A LITTLE SOMETHING FOR EVERYONE

One of the aspects about landscape architecture that Page finds most satisfying is that it offers a challenging way to combine personal interests and passions. For instance, while his personal bent is intensively focused on design, other landscape architects focus more on ecological or historic preservation aspects of the field. One noted colleague is well known for bizarre, surreal garden interpretations such as his bagel park. The history buffs in Page's field help complete pictures of how people used to live by recreating historically accurate gardens and landscaping at national landmarks.

PRACTICING WHAT HE PREACHES

Page's Nashville home is a great example of the magic that a landscape architect can bring to a backyard. Go to your library and find the July 1996 issue of *Southern Living* magazine to see pictures of some of Page's incredible handiwork.

IT'S MORE THAN PLANTING TREES

According to Page, landscape architecture is a wonderful way to leave a lasting contribution to the quality of life for future generations. He views the field as an exceptionally rewarding alternative to some of the more traditional science- and math-oriented professions. It's a profession with a positive job outlook—he'd like to see more bright young people consider it.

Medical Technologist

SHORTCUTS

GO visit a hospital or community laboratory and find out how many tests they run each day.

READ up on the latest diseases and how early testing can sometimes save lives.

TRY making a chart of your family's blood types.

WHAT IS A MEDICAL TECHNOLOGIST?

What happens to the blood sample you give at the doctor's office or the little cup you fill in the doctor's bathroom? They go to a laboratory for medical technologists to test. These medical detectives test blood, urine, body fluids, and tissues to find clues of diseases and other health problems. Doctors and other medical professionals depend on accurate lab work to diagnose and treat many serious illnesses such as AIDS, diabetes, and cancer. Vital test results may often mean a matter of life or death; accuracy is a critical part of this work.

Depending on the size and scope of the lab itself, medical technologists typically work in one or more of five areas in the laboratory, namely

blood bank where technologists are responsible for drawing donor blood, separating blood into its components, and identifying and matching components to insure safe transfusions.

chemistry area where technologists analyze of the chemical composition of blood and body fluids.

hematology area where technologists count, describe, and identify cells in blood and other body fluids (this information helps detect diseases like anemia and leukemia).

immunology area where technologists study biological defenses against viruses or allergy-causing agents.

microbiology area where technologists look for microorganisms such as bacteria, parasites, and fungi.

Tools used in the medical laboratory include microscopes, complex electronic equipment, computers, and other precision instruments, some of which can cost millions of dollars.

To become a medical technologist you'll need to earn a four-year college degree. One particularly interesting option for those pursuing a career as a medical technologist is to work part-time in a medical lab as a medical lab technician while studying to become a technologist. The minimum requirements for a technician can be a high school diploma with some specialized training.

A medical laboratory technician performs general tests working under the direct supervision of a technologist. He or she hunts for clues to the absence, presence, extent, and

causes of disease. It can be a rewarding career in and of itself or as a stepping stone to higher levels of responsibility.

A medical lab technician is a step below a medical technologist in training and responsibility; a pathologist is a step above a technologist. Pathologists are fully trained and accredited medical doctors who specialize in providing and interpreting laboratory information to help diagnose health problems and to monitor the progress of treatment.

Pathologist might be another option to consider in a long-term career plan.

TRY IT OUT

FAVORITE INTERNET HANG-OUTS

One must-see site is Martindale's Health Science Guide's The "Virtual" Medical Center Pathology and Virology Center (http://www-sci.lib.uci.edu/~martindale/HSGuide.html). This site contains an impressive assortment of multimedia exhibits including tutorials, case studies, dictionaries, glossaries, and journals.

There is also an Internet Resources for Pathology and Laboratory Medicine home page that will take you to clinical laboratories and related resources around the world. (http://www.pds.med.umich.edu/users/amp/Path_Resources.html).

FOLLOW THAT BLOOD SAMPLE!

Using information you find on the Internet, resources you dig up from the library, and any helpful advice you can get from professionals, make a chart tracing the path of a typical blood sample from the time it leaves the patient's body to the time the results arrive back at the doctor's office.

Find out who does what, what the routine tests are called, what they are used for, and what kinds of equipment are used. This might not be easy, but it's great practice for developing the detective skills you'll need in the medical lab.

GET IN THE HABIT OF SAVING LIVES

Call the local branch of the American Heart Association or the American Red Cross and find out about the cardiopulmonary resuscitation (CPR) and/or first aid courses that they offer. Although these skills are not part of the lab tech's job description, they'll give you a good introduction to medical practices and the lifesaving importance of following very specific procedures. Good preparation for anyone entering the medical field.

VOLUNTEER AT A BLOOD BANK

Call the American Red Cross or nearby hospitals to find out about any scheduled blood bank drives (a special push to get more blood donors, these are sometimes conducted at businesses, churches, or recreation centers). Tell them you'd like to help out. Your first job may be something along the lines of passing out fruit punch and cookies to revive woozy donors, but you'll meet professionals working in the field and learn more about the work. You'll also find out if you faint at the sight of blood—an important first obstacle to overcome in the medical lab.

CHECK IT OUT

American Society of Clinical Pathologists
2100 West Harrison Street
Chicago, Illinois 60612

Intersociety Committee on Pathology Information
4733 Bethesda Avenue, Suite 700
Bethseda, Maryland 20814

National Accrediting Agency for Clinical Laboratory
   Sciences (NAACLS)
8410 West Bryn Mawr Avenue, Suite 670
Chicago, Illinois 60631

GET ACQUAINTED

Henry C. Lee,
Medical Technologist

CAREER PATH

CHILDHOOD ASPIRATION: To become a doctor.

FIRST JOB: Research assistant in a genetics laboratory.

CURRENT JOB: Technical support specialist at a firm that produces instruments for clinical labs.

Henry C. Lee has been a medical technologist for almost 20 years. He started out in a lab working as a bench technologist. That's someone who actually draws samples and conducts tests. After that, he worked in a university hospital specializing in the chemistry side of things—solving problems and developing new tests. A favorite part of the job for him was the opportunity to teach nearby university students about medical technology. He spent several years as a supervisor in a large clinical lab before switching over to work in a medical equipment corporation.

Lee's new job is a big change from what he's done in the past. The focus is on training lab staff to use sophisticated testing equipment and on trouble-shooting problems with instruments.

WHEN ALL ELSE FAILS, GO TO PLAN B

When Lee started college he had every intention of going on to medical school to become a doctor. However, he made the mistake of spending too much time at the beach and not enough time hitting the books. After the first two years, he realized his grades weren't high enough to get accepted into med school, so he started looking at other options.

He sought the advice of friends and relatives and eventually decided that becoming a medical technologist was a good alternative. After earning a bachelor's degree in microbiology, Lee went through the internship, training, and licensure requirements to become a fully certified medical technologist. It's been the key to an interesting and rewarding career in medicine.

MIND YOUR P'S AND Q'S

In a work environment where thousands of tests can be run every day, Lee says you have to learn to work efficiently and provide consistently correct results. There's a lot at stake when you are talking about a person's health and well-being. Tragic consequences can be the result of careless mistakes. Lee has learned to work like a detective gathering all the clues and tracking down the evidence to give doctors the most reliable results possible.

IF HE HAD TO DO IT ALL OVER AGAIN

He says he'd buckle down and study harder. When you're young, sometimes you don't quite understand how the decisions you make can affect the rest of your life. He learned the hard way how important it is to concentrate and stay focused on what you really want. Although it's easier to let spur-of-the-minute opportunities sway you, it's important to keep sight of the future.

Meteorologist

SKILL SET

✔ SCIENCE

✔ MATH

✔ COMPUTERS

GO visit your local news station and see a weatherperson in action.

READ all you can about clouds, tornadoes, hurricanes, and other weather phenomena.

TRY keeping track of the weather for a week and comparing it with the forecasts in the *Farmer's Almanac*. Were they even close?

WHAT IS A METEOROLOGIST?

True or False? Most meteorologists are the ones on TV giving the weather report. False. Around 90 percent of professional meteorologists are operational and/or research scientists who work behind the scenes to increase the accuracy of forecasts and weather warnings that affect human life. While weather reporting is an important function of meteorology, much work goes on away from the camera to prepare valid weather "news."

The American Meteorologist Society defines meteorologist as a person with specialized education "who uses scientific principles to explain, understand, observe or forecast the earth's atmospheric phenomena and/or how the atmosphere [the air that covers the earth] affects the earth and life on the planet." The primary goal of meteorologists is to completely understand and accurately predict atmospheric phenomena or weather. Lives and livelihood depend on it.

Meteorologists study data on air pressure, temperature, humidity, and wind velocity to make their predictions. They apply physical and mathematical relationships to make short- and long-term weather forecasts. Sophisticated equipment and computer resources such as Doppler radar help make their work more exact. Since the weather business is a 24-hours-a-day, 7-days-a-week operation, someone is always on the watch.

While weather forecasting is one of the best-known applications of meteorology, there are other important applications as well. For instance, some meteorologists work to find ways to control air pollution, others specialize in fields such as agriculture, air and sea transportation, or defense, and still others study trends such as global warming.

Specialties within the field include

Operational meteorology: weather forecasting.

Physical meteorology: study of weather phenomena.

Climatology: analysis of past records of sunshine, wind, rainfall, and temperatures in specific areas.

Research meteorology: in-depth study of specific aspects of meteorology. Research meteorologists have made some important discoveries in the recent past. One of the most exciting and useful outcomes of recent meteorological

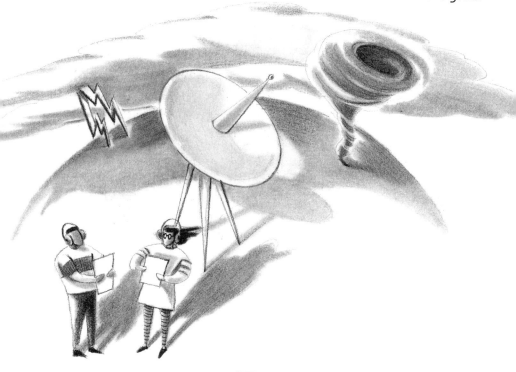

research was the development of an accurate, automatic wind-shear detection and warning system that is now used at major airports all over the United States to provide safer air travel. This safeguard was the direct result of the meteorological study of microbursts.

The National Oceanic and Atmospheric Administration (NOAA) is the largest employer of meteorologists. Meteorologists also work in National Weather Service stations all over the country, for the Department of Defense, and as private weather consultants. And, of course, you'll find a meteorologist or two on staff at most television and radio stations.

TRY IT OUT

NOT FOR THE FAINT-HEARTED

Go to the library and dig up a copy of Aristotle's *Meteorologica*. It was written in 340 B.C. in Greek but has been translated into English and published in a more recent edition. Still, you may find that a book *about* this book is easier to obtain. Make a chart listing various elements of weather: rain, hailstorms, wind, etc. Note what Aristotle said about these things. Now, find a current book on weather. Record current findings on these topics. How many times was Aristotle right?

Ben Franklin, father of the U.S. Weather Bureau, went to great trouble to watch the weather. He flew a kite during a storm to learn about lightning, chased a whirlwind for miles on horseback and tried to break it with his whip, and measured the temperature of the ocean every day on a trip across the Atlantic. To put it mildly, he was an avid weather-watcher. Find out all you can about his work in this arena. Make a chart detailing his discoveries and conclusions.

CLOUD WATCHING

First, draw a picture of clouds from inside without observing them. Next, go outside and compare your picture with the real thing. Then draw a picture of what you see. On the back of each picture, record your observations about the following factors:

- ☀ temperature—Was it hot? Cold?
- ☀ conditions—Was it raining? Snowing? Foggy? Sunny?
- ☀ wind—What direction was it blowing? How strong?

WEATHER STATION

Go to the library and borrow a copy of *The Ben Franklin Book of Easy & Incredible Experiments, Activities, Projects and Science Fun* (A Franklin Institute of Science Museum Book, New York: John Wiley & Sons, Inc., 1995). It gives instructions for making six instruments that will help you observe and forecast the weather.

- ☀ thermometer
- ☀ barometer
- ☀ wind vane
- ☀ anemometer
- ☀ hygrometer
- ☀ rain gauge

Voilà! your own weather station. Use these six instruments to keep track of the weather in your own backyard.

How does fog form? How does the wind blow? How is rain made? How is snowfall measured? Find out in another fascinating book that includes an entire chapter of experiments for the young meteorologist. The book is called *How? More Experiments for the Young Scientist* (Dave Prochnow and Kathy Prochnow. Blue Ridge Summit, Penn.: TAB Books, 1993).

WEATHER-WATCHER

Check the weather forecasts for a week on TV, radio, and the newspaper. Keep a chart and discover which is most accurate.

TANGO WITH AN ON-LINE TORNADO

Learn all you want to know about tornadoes from The Tornado Project Online (http://www.tornadoproject.com). This

website includes fascinating information about recent tornadoes, tornadoes in the past, a top 10 list, and myths and stories. Or write for information on books, video tapes, and posters at P.O. Box 302, St. Johnsbury, Vermont 05819.

CHECK IT OUT

American Meteorological Society
45 Beacon Street
Boston, Massachusetts 02108-3693

American Weather History Center
285 Riverside Drive
Princeton, New Jersey 08540

Association of American Weather Observers
P.O. Box 455
Belvidere, Illinois 61008

Franklin Institute Science Museum
20th and the Parkway
Philadelphia, Pennsylvania 19103-1194

Hurricane Research Division
AOML/NOAA
4301 Rickenbacker Causeway
Miami, Florida 33149

National Climatic Data Center
Federal Building
Asheville, North Carolina 28801

National Severe Storms Laboratory (Tornado)
NOAA/ERL
Norman, Oklahoma 73109

National Weather Service
Public Affairs Office
1325 East-West Highway
Silver Spring, Maryland 20910

GET ACQUAINTED

John Morales, Meteorologist

FOCUSED DETERMINATION

From the time he was a teenager, John Morales knew his life's
work would center around the sky. He considered becoming
a pilot or pursuing a career as an astronomer and finally set-
tled on becoming a meteorologist. With that goal in mind, he
went to the library to look up colleges that provided training
in meteorology. He chose Cornell and graduated in 1984.

HOME SWEET HOME

Born and raised in Puerto Rico, Morales had a job waiting for
him there when he graduated. He spent seven years working
with the National Weather Service in San Juan, Puerto Rico,
Louisiana, and Washington, D.C.

ONE OF A KIND

Morales was the first and is still the only meteorologist in the
United States broadcasting to a Spanish-speaking audience.
There are other Hispanic weather reporters but none with
professional meteorology credentials. He's looking for some
competition!

MOONLIGHTING

Morales is in demand! Along with broadcasting weather reports for four different television shows, he is frequently called to conduct research and provide expert testimony in a highly specialized area of meteorology called forensic meteorology. This involves determining how weather affected past events such as airplane crashes. He also does some weather-related consulting for businesses that need very detailed forecasts, such as ski resorts, agricultural companies, aviation companies, and radio stations.

CONGRATULATIONS!

Morales won a regional Emmy award for his work producing a news video in Spanish called *48 Hours Before the Storm: Step-by-Step Preparation for Hurricanes.* He had plenty of hands-on experience to prepare him for the task. In 1992, during Hurricane Andrew, he spent a solid 25 hours on the air providing warnings and updates on the status of this whopper of a hurricane.

BY THE WAY . . .

Remember that Morales said he had three interests in the sky? Well, to one degree or another, he's fulfilled goals in every area. He's an accomplished meteorologist, he earned his private pilot's license, and he studied some astronomy at Cornell University.

TAKE A TRIP!

Nutritionist

WHAT IS A NUTRITIONIST?

You are what you eat. No one understands the connection between good food and good living better than someone who specializes in the science of nutrition. The very nature of nutritionists' work requires them to be part junk food cop, part healthy food cheerleader. Their job is to prevent and treat diseases through good eating habits.

Another name for nutritionist is dietitian. You'll find dietitians working in many kinds of places, some expected, like hospitals and schools, and some unexpected, like professional sports associations and advertising agencies. The main professional specialties are the following:

Clinical dietitians work in hospitals, clinics, extended care facilities, or nursing homes. They are considered a vital part of the medical team as they develop and monitor nutritional plans to help patients recover from illnesses or to control serious diseases. Some dietitians specialize in a particular area such as nutrition for diabetics, heart patients, or pediatric patients.

Management dietitians work just about anywhere large quantities of food are served: schools, prisons, corporate cafeterias, hotel and restaurant chains, and hospital food service systems. They are responsible for managing staff, planning menus, purchasing food supplies, and maintaining a budget.

Community dietitians help people improve the quality of their lives with proper nutrition. They counsel families, the elderly, pregnant women, children, and disabled or under-privileged people. Community dietitians often augment the staff of child care facilities, government programs, and public health agencies.

Sports and fitness nutritionists are relatively new. These nutritionists work with professional athletes, sports teams, scholastic athlete teams, and individuals to determine the best diet to assure peak performance. In addition to work-ing for professional teams or college and university athlete programs, sports nutritionists can also be employed by health and fitness clubs, gyms, and sports medicine clinics.

TRY IT OUT

SAY HELLO TO THE SIX FOOD GROUPS

The U.S. Department of Agriculture has gone to extreme measures to determine the perfect mix of foods for a healthy human diet. Their findings have been summed up in six basic food groups:

grain	vegetable	meat
fruit	milk	fats, oils, and sweets

Bet you didn't know junk food (fats, oils, and sweets) was on the approved USDA list! It is, but only in moderation and when balanced out with the other food groups.

Make a chart with six columns—one for each food group. Then do the following exercises to get better acquainted with these food groups:

Beginner: Go through your kitchen cabinets, pantry, or refrigerator and list each food item that you find in the proper category.

Amateur: Keep track of the menus served at the school cafeteria for a week. List each food in the appropriate column to determine how well-balanced the meals are.

Expert: Tag along the next time your parent goes to the supermarket. Find five new foods (things you've never tasted before) for each category and write them in the correct column. Ask your parent if you can try one of your discoveries for dinner.

READ ALL ABOUT IT

Pick up a copy of *The American Dietetic Association's Complete Food & Nutrition Guide* (Roberta Larson Duyff. Minnetonka, Minn.: Chronimed Publications, 1996.). It includes more than 600 pages of colorful and readable information about food, health, and nutrition. Save up and buy your own copy or borrow it from your local library.

AN OUNCE OF PREVENTION IS WORTH A POUND OF CURE

Do a little research about some diet-related diseases. Diabetes, heart disease, and cancer are three of the major diseases on which diet has a great effect. Make a list of recommended foods for either preventing the disease or keeping it under control. Using your list of approved foods, plan a healthy menu for breakfast, lunch, and dinner.

Good places to look for information are organizations devoted to finding cures for these diseases. Check the local phone book for a local chapter of the following organizations:

- American Cancer Society
- American Diabetes Association
- American Heart Association

A MENU OF WORLDWIDE OPTIONS

Once again the Internet is the place to be for up-to-the-minute information about dietetics. Of particular interest is the American Dietetic Association website (http://www.eatright.org). From there you can access information about all kinds of nutrition-related issues as well as other organizations.

Next, scoot over to the USDA Food and Nutrition Center homepage at http://www.nal.usda.gov/fnic for information about the six basic food groups and other juicy tidbits.

Just for kicks use a web browser to see what you can find under general categories like food, dietetics, or nutrition.

CHECK IT OUT

American Council of Applied Clinical Nutrition
P.O. Box 509
Florissant, Missouri 63032

American Dietetic Association
Member Services
216 West Jackson Boulevard
Chicago, Illinois 60606-6995
Ask for a copy of *Set Your Sights: Your Future in Dietetics*. The association can also refer you to a member in your state who can answer your questions and share additional materials with you.

Food and Nutrition Center
United States Department of Agriculture
10301 Baltimore Avenue, Room 304
Beltsville, Maryland 20705-2351

GET ACQUAINTED

Leslie Bonci, Registered Dietitian

CAREER PATH

CHILDHOOD ASPIRATION:
Linguist (someone who studies and speaks foreign languages).

FIRST JOB: Researcher for a cancer study about the effects of smoking.

CURRENT JOB: Nutritional consultant.

Leslie Bonci graduated from college with a degree in biopsychology but wasn't sure what to do with her career. She got hooked on the nutrition side of science when she took a nutrition class taught by an especially dynamic woman. The funny thing is her grandmother had told her she'd make a good nutritionist long before she even started considering the field.

FOOTBALL PLAYERS AND BALLERINAS

As part of her private practice, Bonci acts as nutritional consultant for both the Pittsburgh Steelers and the Pittsburgh Ballet Theater. Needless to say, these groups have very different nutritional needs.

She works with individuals helping them plan a diet that will get them to their ideal fighting or dancing weight. She shows them how to shop for food and gives them ideas for preparing food. She also works with the entire football team or corps de ballet, addressing nutrition concerns during training and arranging for appropriate food service when the groups travel. In addition, she works with all the sports teams at the University of Pittsburgh.

THE NUTRITION GAME

Somewhere along the line, sports nutrition became a special niche for Bonci. Her interest in sports nutrition comes naturally though. Bonci is a marathon runner who has discovered firsthand how eating habits help athletic performance. Therefore, motivating athletes to make healthy eating a part of their lifestyle is very important.

NO TIME FOR BOREDOM

As if all this didn't keep Bonci busy enough, she also works in a hospital setting. This work involves helping patients with nutrition-related diseases such as diabetes, colitis, and cancer use the right foods to help keep their medical problems under control. She takes a special interest in helping young people deal with eating disorders like bulimia.

Changing the way Pittsburgh's young people eat is high on her list of priorities, too. Bonci gets involved with various schools in her area and spends volunteer time with students promoting wellness and the prevention of diseases. Her association with the Steelers helps. Kids figure if the big guys listen to her, they might as well do the same.

Oceanographer

SHORTCUTS

GO visit marine life museums and aquariums.

READ about Jacques Cousteau's adventures.

TRY exploring sea life in your own bedroom—start an aquarium.

SKILL SET

✔ ADVENTURE

✔ MATH

✔ SCIENCE

WHAT IS AN OCEANOGRAPHER?

Did you know . . .

- that the ocean covers more than 70 percent of the Earth's surface?
- that within the next 50 years, more than three-quarters of the U.S. population will live within 50 miles of the coastline?
- that the ocean and the seafloor provide important food, minerals, and energy resources for many parts of the world?
- that most international commerce is carried out by marine transport?
- that the ocean influences weather and is a part of the global climate system?

These are just a few of the issues that oceanographers work with every day. Oceanographers apply science and technology to the study of the ocean, its contents, and the surrounding environment through a combination of physics, chemistry, geology, biology, and engineering.

Unsolved questions awaiting the next generation of oceanographers include

- How can we continue to support growing populations near the oceans (with food, recreational resources, etc.) while protecting the coastal waters?
- What role does the ocean play in the development of major (and often devastating) storm systems?
- What kinds of structures can withstand severe storms?
- How can we best preserve and manage seabed resources such as cobalt, chromium, manganese, and platinum?
- In what way can the ocean help delay global warming?

There are various types of oceanographers, specializing in different academic disciplines:

Biological oceanographers study marine plants and animals.

Chemical oceanographers investigate the chemical composition of seawater and its interaction with the atmosphere and the seafloor. The study of trace chemicals helps explain how ocean currents move around the globe.

Geological oceanographers study the ocean floor and map submarine geologic structures to find out more about the history of the earth.

Physical oceanographers investigate the physical dimensions of the ocean such as temperature, density, wave motions, tides, and currents. They often focus on how the ocean interacts with the atmosphere to influence weather and climate.

Needless to say, many oceanographers work near large bodies of water—the Pacific Ocean, the Atlantic Ocean, the Gulf coasts, and the Great Lakes. However, computers and other technology now make it possible to conduct research from laboratories in even the most remote, landlocked areas.

Employment opportunities range from oil and gas research to environmental protection. Other jobs are found in education and training, regulation enforcement, and advisory services.

Oceanography and other marine-related fields appeal to a wide variety of young people. They may seem glamorous and exciting, however, to get the full picture of these professions, you have to include the tedious research and long stretches of data collection that are part of any valid scientific process. If the only impression you have of oceanography is what you've learned from television documentaries, you need to take a good look at this career before deciding if it's right for you.

TRY IT OUT

MAKE YOURSELF SEAWORTHY

Although oceanographers often spend as much time on shore as they do in the water, they need to know how to handle themselves on the water. Take every opportunity you can to get wet and learn about life under the sea. Here are some ideas for starters:

- ♔ Spend a summer (or two or three) working at a marine museum or aquarium. You'll gain valuable experience as well as the opportunity to find out if an underwater career is what you're looking for.
- ♔ Learn how to handle yourself on the water by taking water safety and sailing courses. If you are up for it (and your parents agree) you might even consider spending some time as part of a sailing crew or learning how to scuba dive (under the supervision of well-trained, responsible professionals only, of course).

SAVE YOUR PENNIES FOR SEACAMP

Make the ocean your classroom at one of the highly regarded SEACAMP programs. Based in California and Hawaii, SEACAMP provides marine science education for 7th- to 12th-grade students. These week-long summer camp programs include an invigorating mix of labs, workshops, and research projects as well as exploring tidepools, boogey boarding, scuba-diving, taking field trips on research vessels, and lots more. It's not cheap, but worth every penny if you're looking for a well-rounded introduction to life at sea. Call 800-SEA-CAMP for more information.

FORE OR AFT?

Just to make sure you are sea-savvy before you launch, familiarize yourself with some basic nautical terms and safety procedures. Learning the various flag signals may be another impressive bit of sealore to have under your belt.

FIND OUT ABOUT THE HOT SPOTS

Read all you can about some of the famous diving locations around the world. Start with the Cayman Islands, Hawaii, Washington's San Juan Islands, the Florida Keys, the Blue Hole in Belize, and the Great Barrier Reef in Australia.

STAY AFLOAT

Find out about some of the basic physical laws that effect diving. Dedicate a notebook to your discoveries. Start your search with:

Charles' law   Boyle's law   Dalton's law

DIVE INTO THE INTERNET

Here are a few Internet sites to check out:

☼ Sea World and Busch Gardens put all kinds of information and activities on-line (http://www.seaworld. org/educational_programs/education.html). Get the latest on a variety of species, including baleen whales, bottle-nosed dolphins, manatees, and sharks, or find instructions for some fascinating oceanography experiments.

☼ Find oodles of links to ocean data websites all over the world at http://podaac-www.jpl.nasa.gov/othersources. html.

☼ Greenpeace International can keep you current on environmental programs (http://www.greenpeace. org/).

☼ For all you've ever wanted to know about fish and more look up the National Fisheries Service's Northeast Science Center (http://www.wh.whoi.edu/homepage/ faq.html).

ONE DROP AT A TIME

The following activity is adapted from an on-line experiment offered by Sea World/Busch Gardens. It's a great example of the meticulous research often conducted by oceanographers.

1. Use a stopwatch or clock with a second hand to time how long it takes you to take a shower or bath.
2. Use an empty gallon container to catch water from your bathtub. Time how long it takes to completely fill the container.
3. Divide the time it takes you to shower by the time it took the jug to fill to find out how much water you use for this daily task.
4. Repeat this process for each member of your family. Add all the numbers together to find out how much water your family uses every day to keep clean.
5. Work out a plan to reduce your family's water usage by 25 percent.

6. To get a more complete picture of how much water your family uses, find out how much is used for washing clothes, washing dishes, and watering the lawn. Make a plan to conserve this precious resource.

STRAIGHT TO THE SOURCE

Where does the water in your house come from? Start at the tap and trace its path through pipes to the original water supply. You may need some help from your local city government or utilities company to find out all you need to know. Draw a map that illustrates the path you discover.

READ ALL ABOUT IT

It will cost you a few bucks, but if you want the inside scoop on water-related careers, you'll need to order a copy of *Marine Science Careers: A Sea Grant Guide to Ocean Opportunities*. The booklet profiles an amazing variety of professionals working in marine biology, oceanography, ocean engineering, and related fields. To get information or order a copy write to: Woods Hole Oceanographic Institution, Communications, 193 Oyster Pond Road, CRL 209, Woods Hole, Massachusetts 02543-1525.

CHECK IT OUT

American Geophysical Union
2000 Florida Avenue NW
Washington, D.C. 20009

American Petroleum Institute
1220 L Street NW
Washington, D.C. 20005

Cousteau Society
870 Greenbrier Circle, Suite 402
Chesapeake, Virginia 23320

Marine Technology Society
1825 K Street NW, Suite 203
Washington, D.C. 20006

Oceanography Society
Council of Ocean Affairs
1755 Massachusetts Avenue NW, Suite 700
Washington, D.C. 20036-2102

Scripps Institute of Oceanography
University of California–San Diego
9500 Gilman Drive
Mail Code 0208
La Jolla, California 92093-0208

GET ACQUAINTED

Al Kaltenback,
Chemical Oceanographer

CAREER PATH

CHILDHOOD ASPIRATION:
Wasn't sure, but loved sports, lived by the ocean, and was always blowing up stuff around the house with his chemistry set.

FIRST JOB: Lifeguard at the beach—for six summers.

CURRENT JOB: Advanced chemist for Marathon Oil.

Oceanographer Al Kaltenback and son Liam

A COMMON THREAD

It took a while for Al Kaltenback to catch on, but the ocean played a central role in some of the most important events of his life. He grew up near the ocean and enjoyed six years as a lifeguard at the beach. As soon as he graduated from college, he hitchhiked all the way from New York to California so that he could surf (and work in a gas station After spending some time serving with Uncle Sam (he was drafted during the Vietnam War) and working as a chemist for Marathon, he pursued a graduate degree in oceanography so that he could spend more of his time doing science outdoors.

CRUISING FOR OIL

The earlier years of his career as an oceanographer were spent cruising the Gulf of Mexico developing a scientific method for locating the presence of oil and natural gas without drilling into the ocean floor. This was accomplished by pumping in seawater samples and measuring the various gases. This exploration method was favored by oil companies during the "boom" years of the industry.

More recent years have seen a cutback in this type of exploration. Instead, companies focus on making the best use of existing resources. Now, Kaltenback's work is more likely to involve analyzing rock samples from all over the world to identify hydrocarbons and other elements of mature oil and gas pools. Now the samples come to him and his laboratory in landlocked Colorado instead of him going out to sea to get them.

TWO MONTHS ON A ROLLER COASTER

One of the most exciting (and challenging) oceanography cruises that Kaltenback has taken part in was as an organic geochemist for the Deep Sea Drilling Project. This project involved scientists from all over the world who brought their expertise to explore Earth's structure and history beneath the ocean. From 1968 to 1983 the drillship *Glomar Challenger* logged more than 375,000 miles on 96 voyages across every ocean.

Kaltenback's leg of the cruise involved spending two months in the North Atlantic studying one of the oldest parts

of the continent now under water. This spot is where Greenland, the European mainland, and North America were once connected. His scientific work was made all the more challenging by the almost constant battering the ship took from 30 to 40 foot waves—rough but worth it!

Worth it because the project resulted in several important contributions to human understanding of the Earth. For instance, scientists confirmed a concept called plate tectonics, which helps explain continental movement. They also discovered that the Atlantic seafloor was spreading apart at a rate of more than an inch a year.

CHECK OUT KALTENBACK'S FAVORITE BOOKS

Cosgrove, Stephen. *Harmony: Song of the Sea.* Portland, Oreg.: Graphic Arts Center Publishing Company, 1989.

McNutty, Faith. *How to Dig a Hole to the Other Side of the World.* New York: HarperCollins Children's Books, 1979. This book is written for younger kids, but the illustrations are great. Kaltenback still likes it as an adult scientist. Maybe you'll like it too.

DON'T WORRY IF YOU DON'T KNOW WHAT YOU WANT TO BE YET

Kaltenback knows people who are 50 or 60 years old who still haven't decided what they want to be when they grow up. He says you've got to be flexible enough to adjust to all the changes life will throw at you. Be ready to go with opportunities as they present themselves and do what you think is best at each stage in your life.

Pharmacist

SKILL SET

✔ BUSINESS

✔ MATH

✔ SCIENCE

GO watch the classic holiday movie *It's a Wonderful Life*. Find out what could happen if a pharmacist made a mistake.

READ about Native American natural remedies and other homegrown cures.

TRY thumbing through a medical guide and pronouncing the names of some of the medicines (some of them are real tongue twisters!).

WHAT IS A PHARMACIST?

Pharmacist is a profession that makes frequent appearances in books about top careers for the future. With people living longer and an emphasis on keeping people healthy, opportunities for pharmacists continue to grow at a faster than average pace. Simply put, an increased demand for medicines results in an increased demand for pharmacists to supply them.

The origins of the word *pharmacy* can be traced back to the ancient Greek *pharmakon*, meaning a drug, poison, even spell or charm. However, the profession as we know it today, made its debut in the United States in 1821 with the founding of the first American pharmacy college in Philadelphia.

With expertise in both the scientific and clinical use of medications, the pharmacist is an essential member of the health care team. To be successful, a pharmacist must blend a genuine interest in people and health with a commitment to provide professional, competent care. Computers make it easier for pharmacists to keep track of all the technical information required for the job. However, making that information meaningful and helpful to the many patients they see every day is a skill that must be learned. Educating patients is as much a part of the pharmacist's job as filling prescription orders is.

Typical aspects of a pharmacist's work include curing illnesses; eliminating or reducing symptoms; slowing a disease; preventing disease; diagnosing disease—with minimum risk and maximum comfort for the patient. The basic job description for a pharmacist might include duties such as dispensing prescribed medications, advising patients on their use and possible side effects, recommending over-the-counter drugs, and maintaining accurate records. Checking and double checking are a must when accuracy is often a life or death consideration.

Odds are that you've encountered a pharmacist in the last week or so. Statistics indicate that Americans make over 5 billion trips a year to the pharmacy and that it's not unusual for a pharmacist to see one member of every family in his or her community every week. Odds are even better that your encounter took place in a drug store or community pharmacy since that's where 6 out of 10 pharmacists work.

Other places where pharmacists work include

hospitals where pharmacists work in the hospital pharmacy or practice in a specialized area such as nuclear pharmacy, drug and poison information, or intravenous therapy.

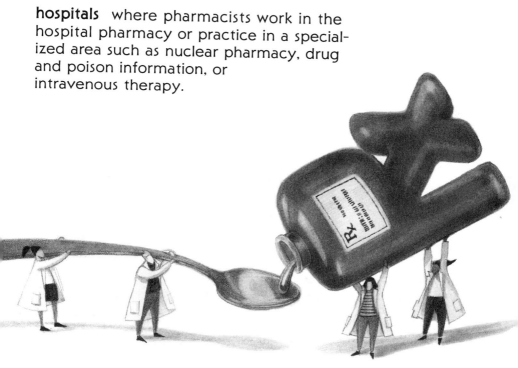

industry where pharmacists work to develop new medications or manufacture health-related products.

government where pharmacists work in a regulatory or public education capacity for federal agencies like the Food and Drug Administration or at the state level as pharmaceutical health inspectors or purchasers.

education where pharmacists teach at the college level to help others prepare for a career in pharmacy.

A doctorate in pharmacy requires four years of professional study, following a minimum of two years of prepharmacy study after high school. It's rigorous but not quite as demanding as some other medical professions.

So, should you be a pharmacist? Here's how the experts at the American Association of Colleges of Pharmacy answer that question: "Yes. You should, if you seek a future in health services and patient care, a professional environment, and a rewarding career where you can use your talents and progress as rapidly as your ability merits."

TRY IT OUT

LEARN THE LINGO

Prescription medications have notoriously tough names to spell and pronounce. Get a sneak peek on the professional terms and figure out some patterns (many of the terms come from Latin) that provide clues to the ingredients by taking a look at the *Physicians Desk Reference* (PDR) (Oradell, N.J.: Medical Economics Co., 1988), the book that pharmacists and physicians rely on. Copies should be available in the reference section of most libraries. Be prepared, this one is really technical so you might want to use it as a starting point to get an idea of pharmaceutical resources.

For a more reader-friendly look at medicines, try books like Harold M. Silverman's *The Pill Book* (New York: Bantam Books, 1982) or the *Complete Guide to Prescription and*

Nonprescription Drugs by H. Winter Griffith (New York: Body Press, 1996).

Find the directory in the back of *The Pill Book* and make a list of all the antihistamines or antibacterial medications. Look up each medication and note the name, recommended dosages, and uses. Make sure to zero in on word clues that help define its use in treating specific kinds of illnesses or germs.

Take your search a little further by using a computer to link up with Martindale's Virtual Pharmacy (http://www-sci.lib.uci.edu/~martindale/Pharmacy.html) on the Internet. Here's your chance to learn more than you ever wanted to know about specific medications.

WHAT'S THAT TREE DOING IN THE MEDICINE CABINET?

Some of the best ingredients for medicines grow on trees. Really. Go to the library or check out the Internet to find out all you can about nature's healing touch. Some resources to look for include

---

Althschel, Siri von Reis. *Drugs and Foods from Little Known Plants.* Cambridge, Mass.: Harvard University Press, 1973.

Crellin, John R. and Jane Philpott. *Herbal Medicine Past and Present.* Durham, N.C.: Duke University Press, 1990.

Foster, Steven and James Duke. *A Field Guide to Medicinal Plants.* Boston: Houghton Mifflin, 1990. This one includes lots of pictures!

You may also want to write to the World Resources Institute, 1709 New York Avenue NW, Washington, D.C. 20006, to request information. This organization conducts a good deal of pharmaceutical and pharmacological research.

TAKE A GUIDED TOUR

An Internet site you'll want to visit is http://www.herbweb.com. Here you'll find an introduction to herbal medicines. Find out about typical work days and duties of pharmacists in

nearly every practice field in *The Pfizer Guide: Pharmacy Career Opportunities*, a 355-page book of articles on career opportunities available to pharmacists. To obtain a free copy, contact your local school of pharmacy or request one from Merritt Communications, 142 Ferry Road, Suite 13, Old Saybrook, Connecticut 06475.

Another good resource is *Opportunities in Pharmacy Careers*. Find it in your library or order a copy from National Textbook Company, 4255 West Touhy Avenue, Lincolnwood, Illinois 60646.

OH, MY ACHING HEAD!

Find the nonprescription medication aisle at the grocery store. First, look at all the aspirin-like medications. Note the different symptoms the medication is supposed to treat on the labels. See if you can determine the "magic ingredient" that makes each one work the way it does. Also, note the differences in dosage and prices. Make a chart to record your findings. If someone asked you for the most effective and least expensive remedy for a headache, what would you recommend?

CHECK IT OUT

American Association of Colleges of Pharmacy
CIC Coordinator
1426 Prince Street
Alexandria, Virginia 22314

American College of Apothecaries
205 Daingerfield Road
Alexandria, Virginia 22314

American Pharmaceutical Association
2215 Constitution Avenue NW
Washington, D.C. 20037

American Society of Consultant Pharmacists
1321 Duke Street
Alexandria, Virginia 22314

American Society of Hospital Pharmacists
7272 Wisconsin Avenue
Bethesda, Maryland 20814

National Association of Chain Drug Stores
P.O. Box 1417-D49
413 North Lee Street
Alexandria, Virginia 22313

Pharmaceutical Research and Manufacturers of America
1100 15th Street NW
Washington, D.C. 20005

GET ACQUAINTED

Anthony Conte, Pharmacist

FIRST GENERATION COLLEGE GRAD

Anthony Conte's father came to America as an infant with his brother and sister because their parents had died. Times were tough and they struggled to survive in their new country. Conte's father never had the opportunity to go to school, so he taught himself to read and write. He eventually owned his own business and made a nice living for his family. However, he learned to appreciate the value of an education and made certain that his only son, Anthony, made the most of his opportunities.

CAREER PATH

CHILDHOOD ASPIRATION: To become an engineer because he liked to draw mechanical illustrations of structures like bridges.

FIRST JOB: Started working in a pharmacy after school at the age of nine and stayed there until he graduated from high school.

CURRENT JOB: Mostly retired, occasional pharmaceutical consultant and painter of wildlife art.

It should come as no surprise that young Conte was first in his class in grammar school and high school. During his senior year, his father noticed a newspaper advertisement for a local university that said "become a professional pharmacist in 4 years." He decided that the program sounded like a good idea for his son, and fortunately Anthony agreed. Having spent several years working in a pharmacy—sweeping floors at first and gradually moving up to delivering prescriptions and helping customers—Conte liked the idea of becoming a pharmacist.

As it turns out, those early days in the pharmacy helped shape the pharmacist he would later become. One man in particular, Ray DiPiola, stands out as the ethical, generous person of principle that Conte worked to emulate in his own business dealings.

THOSE WERE THE DAYS

When Conte enrolled in classes at Long Island University's College of Pharmacy in 1948, tuition was just $422 per year. It cost him a nickel each way for transportation from his home to school and back.

Conte earned his bachelor's degree in pharmacy and went on to obtain a master's degree in pharmaceutical chemistry from Columbia University. He won an American Foundation Fellowship to pursue a doctorate at the University of Florida, but Uncle Sam preempted those plans with a military draft notice.

When Conte completed his military duty, he got married and opened a drug store in New York City in 1955. It just so happened that he shared a building with doctors that specialized in treating ear, nose, and throat problems. Located not far from Broadway, the doctors helped many famous stars keep their voices in shape for nightly performances. Conte eventually developed a special gargle that numbed the throat and reduced swelling in the membranes. It became a "voice-saver" for Broadway stars like Ethel Merman, Paul Newman, and Montgomery Cliff.

NOW THAT'S SERVICE!

After being held up at gunpoint six times in seven months, Conte decided it was time to move out of the city. He found more than he had hoped for in Great Neck, New York. There he discovered a state-of-the art pharmacy that had been started by the Gilliar brothers in the 1920s. Offering home delivery by horse and carriage before there were roads in town, the brothers quickly made exceptional service the hallmark of their store.

The tradition of exceptional customer service continued under Conte's leadership, and the store was open every day of the year from 8:00 A.M. to 10:00 P.M. Conte made it a point to get to know his customers and to take the time to answer their questions about everything from health concerns to marital problems and financial decisions. His commitment to service even extended past working hours. It wasn't unusual to get a phone call at 1 A.M. or 2 A.M. from a frantic parent tending to a suddenly ill child. Conte never hesitated to open the store, fill the prescription, and deliver it even in the wee hours of the night.

Anthony Conte's
"state-of-the-art" pharmacy

THE FAMILY THAT WORKS TOGETHER . . .

Conte often enlisted the help of his family in the store. His wife, Helen, also a pharmacist, worked behind the counter. His daughter, Lisa, became the resident cosmetologist, helping customers in the cosmetics department. His son, Charles, made deliveries.

This early introduction to the medical world paid off. Today, Charles is a surgeon, and Lisa is the CEO of San Francisco–based Shaman Pharmaceuticals, a company that adapts cures used by traditional rainforest healers for use in modern, plant-based medicines.

DON'T FORGET THE MATH

You can't do science without math, Conte advises. Skills like solving equations, making extractions, and drawing conclusions all come into play in the science of pharmacy. He also urges future pharmacists to do their homework by learning all you can about new medicines and treatments.

GET SOME RESPECT

During his 36 years in the business, Conte found pharmacy to be a well-respected and satisfying profession. He, like many other pharmacists, made a valuable contribution to his community and enjoyed helping the people in his neighborhood. A Gallup poll indicated that many Americans agree: For several years running, pharmacy has been named as one of the most respected professions in America.

Robotics Technician

SKILL SET

✔ COMPUTERS

✔ MATH

✔ SCIENCE

GO nose around town and find some ways robots are used in industry. Ask if you can see it in action.

READ some of Isaac Asimov's science fiction books, such as *I, Robot*.

TRY catching some reruns of Lost in Space or the Star Trek movies for ideas about fictional robots.

WHAT IS A ROBOTICS TECHNICIAN?

Wouldn't it be great to have a robot that could clean your room, do you homework, and wash the dishes? So far, one with these skills hasn't been created, but you can be sure someone is working on it!

Robots are mechanical devices that perform tasks so that people don't have to; many seem to think like humans. Note that they only *seem* to think like humans. So far, people do the thinking for robots and must program their activity down to the most minute detail. Scientists and computer experts around the world are racing to be the first to develop a robot that can think on its own and make decisions. (Maybe you'll be the one to invent such a robot!)

Robotic technicians help engineers and other industrial scientists design, develop, produce, test, operate, and repair robots and robotic devices. In the field of robotics there are three specialties:

Artificial intelligence (AI) is the specialty in which scientists are attempting to find mechanical or electronic ways to mimic human intelligence capabilities. Scientists generally work in one of four general areas of research: pattern recognition, problem-solving, information representation, and natural language interpretation.

Technology is the specialty devoted to designing mechanical devices for maneuvering and manipulating. One of the goals of technology is to develop movement capabilities that function reliably and consistently without external control.

Computer programming is the specialty that involves teaching robots to communicate and follow commands. There's a smart computer programmer behind every smart computer and a smart computer behind every smart robot.

Many of the technological advances in this field have been in industries where robots are used to perform tasks once associated with assembly line labor, particularly in the automotive industry. Robots are often used to do work that would be dangerous, uncomfortable, incredibly boring, or even impossible for humans to do.

The best robotic technicians are scientifically minded and mechanically inclined. That's because the work can involve actually putting together very technical gizmos and keeping them running. Make sure to include some machine-shop skills and drafting with your math and science courses.

Whatever you do, make sure that any robots you work with adhere to Asimov's laws of robots. These three laws govern the ethics of robotic experts around the world.

☆ A robot may not injure a human being or through inaction allow a human being to come to harm, unless this would violate a higher order law.

☆ A robot must obey orders given it by human beings, except where such orders would conflict with a higher order law.

☆ A robot must protect its own existence, as long as such protection does not conflict with a higher order law.

TRY IT OUT
GO AT IT WITH GUSTO

Robotics International sponsors an annual Student Robot Contest in which groups of students across the United States and from Canada compete in creating robots that handle tasks like picking up and placing objects, navigating through a maze, or robot construction. The process requires teamwork and a sponsor. For information write to RI/SME Student Robot Contest, 1 SME Drive, P.O. Box 930, Dearborn, Michigan 48121.

FRIDAY NIGHT AT THE MOVIES

Your teacher can request a free copy of *Adventures in Manufacturing* from the Society of Manufacturing Engineers (see Check It Out). This video consists of three segments: a 23-minute introduction to "The Challenge of Manufacturing," a 28-minute segment called "Race Against Time" in which engineers and engineering students talk about the financial and personal rewards of their career choice, and a 13-minute description of all the ways engineering touches our lives—everything from jet fighters and rock and roll music to make-up, clothes, and cars.

ROBO-PALS

It's so incredible! You, sitting in front of a computer and modem, with a few clicks of a mouse can control robots around the world (by remote control, that is). How about an ASEA 6 industrial robot in Australia? Perhaps bossing a robot in Singapore sounds more exotic. Maybe a telescope is more your style or a chance to draw on an art gallery floor. It's all there and more at a site devoted exclusively to the Web's entertaining and educational robotic websites. Explore it at http://telerobot.mech.uwa.edu.au.

Visit several sites and make a poster that illustrates the different robots and their functions. Rate them according to fun (Did you enjoy working with it?), function (How sophisticated was its task?), and form (How well did it perform?).

TAKE ME TO YOUR LEADER

For a small investment you can build a six-legged walking robot named Stiquito that fits in the palm of your hand. It uses an unusual nickel-titanium alloy called nitintol that directly converts the energy of a 9-volt battery into mechanical force. You can order a kit from Computer Science Department, Attention Stiquito, 215 Lindley Hall, Indiana University, Bloomington, Indiana 47405. A how-to video is also available.

CHECK IT OUT

American Institute of Aeronautics and Astronautics
370 L'Enfant Promenade SW
Washington, D.C. 20024

Association for Unmanned Vehicle Systems
1735 North Lynn Street, Suite 950
Arlington, Virgina 22209

Robotics and Automation Council
Institute of Electrical and Electronic Engineers (IEEE)
Education Information
345 East 47th Street
New York, New York 10017

Robotics Industries Association
900 Victors Way
P.O. Box 3724
Ann Arbor, Michigan 48106

Society of Manufacturing Engineers
Education Department
1 SME Drive
P.O. Box 930
Dearborn, Michigan 48121

GET ACQUAINTED

Richard Lefebvre, Robotics Engineer

CAREER PATH

CHILDHOOD ASPIRATION: He was intrigued by all things electrical and actually pursured a degree in electronics.

FIRST JOB: A stockboy in a hardware store during high school.

CURRENT JOB: Project manager of advance product and process technology for a leading manufacturer of automotive structural components.

Richard Lefebvre got into robotics over 30 years ago—just when things started hopping. His work includes robotic advances in the areas of factory automation, systems integration, application engineering, and technical support. Since 1971, he has been directly involved in developing more than 600 welding and material handling robots. He named the first few, after a while it was too hard to keep track of all of them.

HE'S GOOD AT WHAT HE DOES, REAL GOOD

In 1993, Lefebvre (out of every robotics engineer in the world) was named recipient of the Joseph F. Engelberger International Robotic Award for his impressive contributions to the advance of robotics in industry. The award is named after the father of robotics, the man credited with developing and patenting one of the first robots.

IT'S ALWAYS NEW

Lefebvre thrives on the challenge of his work. It is always changing, and he's learned to stay on top of new developments by reading journals, attending trade shows and conferences, and staying in touch with colleagues all over the world.

ADVICE TO THE NEXT GENERATION OF ROBOTICS PROS

Education, education, education. There's no way around it. The technology has become so sophisticated that a solid education is the cornerstone of success in this field. Learn how to learn and how to think things through; these skills can take you anywhere.

Science Educator

WHAT IS AN EDUCATOR?

That's a question you might be better qualified to answer than adults are. As a student, you are surrounded by educators every day. Classroom teachers, textbook writers, educational software designers, and more. If you stop and think about it you could probably write a job description defining the qualities of a really good teacher. You could probably write a pretty accurate description of a really bad teacher too—everyone seems to get their share of both.

As far as job opportunities go, education is a field in which things are expected to be booming as your generation enters the workforce. By the year 2002, America's school-age population is expected to be double what it was in 1986. That means there will be twice as much opportunity in elementary and secondary schools, both public and private. Colleges, vocational schools, and adult continuing education programs are other sources of teaching careers.

In addition, new technology such as educational software, the World Wide Web, and multimedia materials has created some interesting niches that provide educators with options in addition to actually teaching in a classroom.

Of course, there will always be a need for well-trained, highly motivated, committed teachers to work in classrooms

for all ages—preschool through advanced college degrees. The old saying that "if you can't do it, teach it" is completely out of sync with our modern world. The educational needs of modern society require instructors who are the cream of the crop in every way—as communicators, as subject experts, and as worthy role models.

This is how the American Federation of Teachers describes the job of teaching: ". . . it's difficult, wonderful, exhausting, fun, stressful, enlightening—and rewarding beyond compare. Teaching requires enormous patience. Good teachers are fair to their students, they are interested in ideas, they believe that teaching and learning are important. They have a strong commitment to democracy and social progress. Good teachers want to make a difference."

Science teachers, in particular, tend to be a highly specialized group. The focus is generally on life sciences, chemistry, or physics. The older the audience, the more specialized the class content. For instance, in some high schools and in most colleges, instructors may teach courses in astronomy, genetics, or biochemistry. It is especially necessary that science teachers stay current in their fields by reading about new discoveries and theories in professional journals, participating in workshops and continuing education opportunities, and keeping up with technological advances.

So, what do you think? Are you ready to don a lab coat and introduce others to the mysteries of science?

TRY IT OUT

PEER PRESSURE

Many schools offer peer counseling or tutoring programs that involve students in helping other students. Find out if your school or a nearby elementary school offers any programs like this and sign up for training.

RUG RATS, INC.

Child care centers, recreation centers, and summer day-camp programs can be a great training ground for aspiring educators. Some public libraries also use young teens as assistants in programs that promote reading among children. Find out about volunteer opportunities or part-time jobs in programs that serve little people.

You'll learn more and enjoy the experience more if you link up with a good program. Ask your parents, a teacher, or a school counselor to help you check out the program's credentials and reputation before you commit yourself to spending time there.

Another option is to offer baby-sitting services to neighbors and relatives. Put together a bag of tricks to entertain the children, actually plan some interesting age-appropriate activities for your young charges, and watch your savings account grow with your earnings. (A hint from an experienced employer of baby-sitters: Clean up your messes and do the dishes; you'll get paid more and be asked back again!)

EXPERTS JOURNAL

Pick a topic that you'd like to know more about: clouds, ecosystems, something scientific. Find all the materials about this topic that you can (look in the children's section, young adult section, and general nonfiction section of the library; ask your teachers for suggestions; check out Internet resources). In short, become a miniexpert on your topic. Record your findings in a notebook.

Next, make a plan for how you could share this information in a way that would be meaningful and memorable to a younger audience. Make visuals, design experiments, and out-line a verbal presentation. Put your lesson together in a way that you would prefer for your own school lessons—lively, fun, interesting. Get some neighborhood kids together or recruit your younger siblings and put your teaching skills to the test.

CYBERSCHOOL

Science education is a happening spot on the Internet. Go on-line and hook up with the Science Education Gateway (SEGway) (http://www.cea.berkeley.edu/Education). Depending on your keyboard skills, you can probably reach them just as quickly by typing their name in a web browser. This site includes ready-made classroom activities for kindergarteners through 12th graders as well as images, interactive tools, text, and other resources to help you build your own Internet-based science classroom.

Go through several topics and note carefully how each lesson is put together—the instructions, the information, the activities, the questions, etc. Compare how materials are presented for younger children, middle schoolers, and high schoolers.

Using some of the organizational techniques you observed in the on-line lessons and the information you gathered for your Experts Journal, develop an on-line lesson plan. Make your lesson one that you'd want to sit in on if you were a student in that grade: focused, fun, and interesting.

CHECK IT OUT

American Federation of Teachers
555 New Jersey Avenue NW
Washington, D.C. 20001-2079

Association of School, College and University Staffing (ACUS)
1600 Dodge Avenue, S-330
Evanston, Illinois 60201
This association publishes the *Job Search Handbook for Educators*, an informative overview of job search strategies, a breakdown of geographic and curriculum areas that are most in demand, and

actual ads from school districts. The guide can be ordered from the association for a small fee but may be available at your local library.

National Education Association
1201 16th Street NW
Washington, D.C. 20036

Recruiting New Teachers
385 Concord Avenue, Suite 100
Belmont, Massachusetts 02178
800-45-TEACH
This group provides brochures and copies of *The Careers in Teaching Handbook*, a free, in-depth guidebook that covers just about everything you'd want to know about a career in teaching.

GET ACQUAINTED

Steve Spangler, Science
Teacher/Speaker/Inventor

CAREER PATH

CHILDHOOD ASPIRATION: A television game show host.

FIRST JOB: Disc jockey for wedding receptions and school dances.

CURRENT JOB: Nationally known science speaker, author, and lecturer.

If you ever get the chance to meet Steve Spangler, you'll never forget it. He's one of those guys who makes a lasting impression wherever he goes. He's funny. He's smart. He loves what he does. And it shows.

Spangler has two vocational passions, science and teaching, and he's found some exciting ways to combine the two into a truly unique career. Here's a list of some of the ways he does this:

💡 as host of the "Wonder Why?" science segment on
News for Kids, a nationally syndicated children's television program
💡 as author of science activity books like *Taming the
Tornado Tube: 50 Weird and Wacky Things You Can Do
With A Tornado Tube!*, and *Down to a Science*
💡 as presenter of science assembly programs (he's talked
to more than a quarter of a million students!)
💡 as creator of a popular line of science activities and science kits
💡 as a trainer for teachers
💡 as leader of summer science camps

BLOOD AND GUTS

After his parents and teachers convinced him that there was-
n't a big job market for game show hosts, Spangler started
warming to the idea of becoming a doctor. He took all the
right courses in high school and even landed a position as
assistant to an ophthalmologist. He was on his way to hang-
ing out a shingle that read *Steve Spangler, M.D.* The only
problem—which he fortunately discovered sooner rather
than later—was that he couldn't stand the sight of blood. This is
a small but very significant detail for a doctor—time for plan B.

Spangler says that this experience taught him an important
lesson that you need to know too: You never know if a career
is right for you unless you try it! People learn best by doing!

THERE'S MORE THAN ONE WAY TO GET THERE!

Spangler graduated from college with a degree in chemistry.
His plan was to start teaching at his old high school. Things
were in upheaval at the school when he graduated, so his
mentor advised him not to start teaching there. In fact, she
advised him not to become a teacher at all but to consider
becoming a chemist. Now what?

Spangler and his wife talked about the best next step.
Spangler knew he didn't want to work as a chemist in a laboratory, so they looked at what he really enjoyed. Chemistry,

teaching, magic, and interacting with people were high on the list. The next step was figuring out how he could make a living doing those things. The result was sending out brochures to schools offering to come in and "turn kids on to science."

Things took off from there—school presentations, the television show, the first books, the science camp programs—and Spangler had created his own custom-made career as a science "edutainer."

THE SQUIDY STORY

Spangler showed up on his first day of kindergarten with a science toy that he and his father had made for show-and-tell. It was something called a Cartesian diver—an eye dropper in a bottle of water that would float and sink simply by squeezing the bottle. Almost 25 years later, Spangler remembered his kindergarten experience and decided to use the floating and sinking eye dropper on his television program.

There was one unforeseen problem. The television camera had a hard time focusing on the eye-dropper—it was too hard to see in the bottle. After spending countless hours wandering around department stores and hobby shops, he stumbled across a device resembling a fishing lure that could be attached to the hard-to-see eye dropper. It made the eye-dropper look like a swimming squid. Spangler nicknamed it "Squidy" and took his idea back to his television producer.

Shortly after the segment aired on *News for Kids*, Spangler started receiving phone calls from viewers (mostly teachers) who were interested in purchasing "Squidy." Unfortunately, the rubber squidlike creatures that Spangler found in the fishing store were not quite big enough to fit over the eye dropper. So, he contacted a prominent fish lure manufacturer to see if they could make a special batch of rubber squid lures just for this experiment. After many confusing telephone conversations with the manufacturer (they couldn't understand anyone would want a fishing lure that wasn't intended to catch a fish!), they agreed on a price for the mold and the price of each rubber squid. The key, of course, was that

Spangler had to purchase the little squids in quantity, as the manufacturer pointed out. How hard could it be to sell a few hundred Squidy Cartesian Diver toys?

Unfortunately, there was a communication breakdown on one tiny, little detail, and that was in the use of the term *quantity*. Steve assumed that *quantity* meant 500 or so. . . .

About three weeks after Steve placed the order, he found a surprise waiting for him on his driveway. It seems that a delivery truck dropped by earlier in the day and unloaded 80,000 rubber squids in boxes. Of course, with every delivery comes a bill—the bigger the delivery, the bigger the bill. Yikes!

It's one thing to come up with a clever idea for a science toy, but marketing and selling the toy proved to be the real challenge for Steve and his wife, Renee. After many months of hard work, a crash course in marketing and packaging, and frequent trips to trade shows around the country, Squidy had become one of the top selling science toys in the country.

Today, Squidy is available in over 1,000 stores and nearly 2,000 catalogs worldwide. It's a classic example of making lemonade out of the lemons life sometimes throws you!

THE SECRET OF SPANGLER'S SUCCESS

Spangler has been fortunate; throughout his life there have been special people who have helped guide him along the way. There was the ophthalmologist for whom he worked, his boss when he was a DJ, a very special teacher in high school, and wonderful parents who helped focus his energy. All these people took him under their wings, shared their experience, and taught him important lessons that helped prepare him for what he's doing now. Of course, the key to the success of these mentoring relationships was that he actually listened and used what he learned.

FAMOUS LAST WORDS

In his motivational presentations, Steve tells young people, "Don't tell me what you can do. Tell me what you love to do, and I'll tell you what you should do for the rest of your life. Take a risk and enjoy your success. Take a risk and fail miserably. Learn from every failure as you strive to reach your next goal. That's success!"

Veterinarian

WHAT IS A VETERINARIAN?

A veterinarian should have a love of animals, but it doesn't stop there. A veterinarian has to know as much about animals as a medical doctor knows about humans. In fact, the jobs are very similar. Animals get sick just like humans do. Animals get hurt in accidents just like humans do. Veterinarians are doctors who care for animals.

Most veterinarians care for companion animals, or pets, such as dogs, cats, and birds. Many run their own private clinics and carry the same responsibilities as other business owners and employers. In addition, a typical day at a clinic might involve immunizing a dozen dogs of various breeds, neutering or spaying a cat or two, performing emergency surgery on an animal that's been hit by a car, and setting some broken bones.

If the vet specializes in larger animals, his or her time might be spent at a farm, ranch, or zoo helping birth a new lamb, immunizing an entire herd of cattle, or giving nature a hand by artificially inseminating a horse. While most of their work is done during regular business hours, both types of vets must be ready to respond to middle-of-the-night emergencies.

Most of the routine tasks performed by a vet can be summed up in two categories: doing things to keep animals healthy—regular checkups, shots, and tests—and doing things to help sick animals get better—diagnosing diseases, prescribing medication, performing surgery, treating injuries.

While most veterinarians care for pets and farm animals in animal hospitals or clinics, other vets

- care for animals used in sporting events, such as horse races
- care for laboratory animals used in scientific studies
- care for zoo or aquarium animals
- specialize in areas like surgery, anesthesiology, microbiology, and pathology

Another option for veterinarians is public health work. These vets work for federal agencies like the Food and Drug Administration or the Centers for Disease Control, as well as state and local agencies. Some of the responsibilities of vets in public health might include

- protecting humans against diseases carried by animals
- inspecting livestock and foods
- conducting research and testing biological products such as vaccines

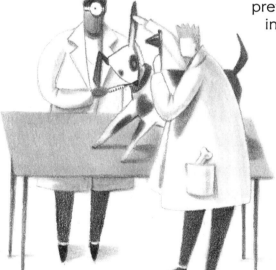

- evaluating new drugs to prevent or treat diseases in humans and animals

The major difference between private practice and public practice is the patient. In private practice the patients are individual animals or groups of animals with specific problems that the vet works to solve. In public practice, the patient is the entire community, and the vet's job is to safeguard overall health and well-being in simple and sometimes very complex ways.

For instance, one of the main tasks of the U.S. Department of Agriculture (USDA) is to protect people's food sources. This involves making sure that food derived from animals is safe to eat and inspecting food processing plants. However, when an outbreak of some food-borne disease occurs (for example, an illness caused by *E.coli*), these veterinarians are among the detectives tracing tainted sources and remedying the problem.

Veterinarians must complete a rigorous college program to earn their doctorate degree in veterinary medicine. This training takes six to eight years to complete. Veterinary technician is another option that requires only a two-year associate's degree. Veterinary technicians assist vets in many ways including caring for hospitalized patients, conducting routine laboratory tests, taking X rays, and assisting in surgical procedures.

Unlike the fictional Dr. Doolittle, most of the communicating that vets do is with people. They must be prepared to share the joy of a new litter of pups as well as the sorrow of euthanizing a dearly loved, hopelessly sick pet. It's important work. Just ask anyone who has ever loved a pet.

TRY IT OUT

NOAH'S NOTEBOOK

The flood lasted more than one night and so will this project. But, if you want to make animals the center of your career, you're going to have to start boning up on them. Get a three-ring notebook and some dividers. Stop and think before you do the next part.

How you organize will depend on how deeply you want to delve into the animal kingdom. You can divide the notebook according to categories of animals: companion animals (pets), large domesticated animals (farm and ranch animals), exotic animals (reptiles and birds), and zoo animals. Or you can get more specific with individual species: an entire section devoted to dogs, cats, horses, etc. You decide and get it organized.

Next, you'll want to find out all you can about these animals and write down the details. Find or draw a picture to include with each summary. Make sure to include information about feeding and breeding habits, life expectancy, and common personality traits.

The library, of course, can be a great source of information. Get on-line at the NetVet site and check out the Electronic Zoo for some fun information and photos (see Sniff Out below for details).

Keep working on this project bit by bit until you've compiled as many animal facts as you can. Try not to get bogged down—after all it's just a notebook. Just think what it must have been like for Noah. You can bet that Noah sometimes wished all he had to take care of was a notebook!

SNIFF OUT INTERNET RESOURCES

Aspiring vets should take a peek at the *I Want to Be a Veterinarian* interactive career magazine on the World Wide Web (http://www.futurescan.com/vet!). Published and provided free of charge by FutureScan, this website includes feature articles, interviews, day-in-the-life tours, an advice column, and reference materials. It's interactive and fun!

Also, use a web browser to find NetVet. This site is full of useful information and provides links to all kinds of interesting veterinary resources. It also includes the Electronic Zoo. Visit regularly to read best animal-related sites on the Web in the Pick of the Litter.

STRAIGHT FROM THE HORSE'S MOUTH

Find out what it's really like to be a vet by reading books written by veterinarians about various aspects of their profession. Some are written for children, can be a good place to start learning about a new area, and often have lots of neat pictures. Here are a few suggested by some librarians from veterinarian schools.

Drum, Sue. *Women in Veterinary Medicine: Profiles of Success.* Ames, Iowa: Iowa State University Press, 1991.

Frye, Frederic. *Phyllis, Phallus, Genghis Cohen & Other Creatures I Have Known.* Melbourne, Fla.: Krieger Publishing Co., 1995.

Gage, Loretta, and Nancy Gage. *If Wishes Were Horses.* New York: St. Martin's Press, 1993.

Gasofer, Seymour. *In Sickness and in Love.* Virginia Beach, Va.: Donning, 1980.

Haddock, Sally. *The Making of a Woman Vet.* New York: Simon and Schuster, 1985.

Hanley, Frank H. *A Veterinary Odyssey.* Hicksville, N.Y.: Exposition Press, 1978.

Miller, Robert M. *Most of My Patients Are Animals.* Middlebury, Vt.: P.S. Eriksson, 1985.

Porter, James A. *Doctor, Matilda's in Labor.* Ames, Iowa: Iowa State University Press, 1986.

Taylor, David. *Going Wild: Adventures of a Zoo Vet.* New York: Stein and Day, 1981.

————. *Is There a Doctor in the Zoo?* Philadelphia: Lippincott, 1978.

————. *Next Panda, Please.* New York: Stein and Day, 1983.

Ware, Jean, and Hugh Hunt. *The Several Lives of a Victorian Vet.* New York: St. Martin's Press, 1980.

ANIMAL KEEPER FOR HIRE

Get some firsthand experience caring for animals. You need to know how well you can handle the responsibility and how much you enjoy it. The experience will also help you when it comes time to apply to vet school; it is considered a plus. A few suggestions of where you could get some experience are

- ☼ at a pet store, vet's office, farm, ranch, horse stable, or zoo (be prepared for some of the dirty work—it comes with the territory) doing part-time work.
- ☼ at an animal shelter on a volunteer basis or, if your parents agree, with an animal foster care program like MAXFund.
- ☼ at a local 4-H group—most of these offer a variety of animal care programs.

CHECK IT OUT

American Veterinary Medical Association
1931 North Meacham Road, Suite 100
Schaumburg, Illinois 60173-4360
Send a large self-addressed stamped envelope with a request for
a copy of *Today's Veterinarian*.

Association of American Veterinary Medical Colleges
1101 Vermont Avenue NW, Suite 710
Washington, D.C. 20005-3521

North American Veterinary Technician Association
P.O. Box 224
Battle Ground, Indiana 47290

GET ACQUAINTED

Dr. Michael Blackwell,
Veterinarian

CAREER PATH

CHILDHOOD ASPIRATION: To be a vet.

FIRST JOB: Reopened his father's veterinary clinic in Oklahoma.

CURRENT JOB: Veterinarian in private practice and in public health.

Wow! Dr. Michael Blackwell enjoys a distinguished career as a veterinarian. Not only does he operate a private practice in a clinic located right next to his house, he is also deputy director of the Center for Veterinary Medicine of the U.S. Food and Drug Administration (FDA) and chief veterinarian of the U.S. Health Service. Fortunately, an associate helps run the clinic when Blackwell is busy serving as the nation's "top vet."

IN HIS FATHER'S FOOTSTEPS

Blackwell's father was a veterinarian, and Blackwell remembers following him around the clinic every chance he got from as early as he can remember. The only time he considered any profession other than veterinarian was in his senior year in high school when a career day recruiter enticed him with the notion of making big bucks with just a couple years of engineering training. It was tempting but not enough to lure him away from fulfilling his lifetime dream of becoming a vet. After graduating from college in Alabama, he returned to Oklahoma and doctored pets and farm animals in what had been his father's practice. Talk about tough shoes to fill!

NEVER SAY NEVER

Blackwell enjoys working directly with animals and is especially honored by the trust his patient's owners place in him. He eventually reached the point in his career where he wanted to help people on a larger scale. Through an interesting series of events, he ended up pursuing a degree in public health, an aspect of the field he found so uninteresting while in vet school as to snooze through presentations about public practice opportunities.

As fate would have it, working for the FDA is where everything has come together for him. He works indirectly with animals, yet his work affects millions of people every day—even you. Did you realize that 25 cents out of every dollar you spend is spent on something regulated by the FDA?

THE DAYS GET PRETTY LONG

Wearing as many hats as he does, Blackwell keeps on the run. He usually starts the day with some time in the clinic—getting organized, checking on overnight "guests," and whatever else needs his immediate attention. It's not unusual for him to be in the first of many meetings at his FDA office by 7:30A.M. Much of his day is spent solving problems. The difference between these problems and the ones he faces at the clinic is that these problems have already gone through a lot of smart people before they get to him. It can be a real challenge to find the best solutions.

He often represents the FDA at conferences with product manufacturers, veterinary associations, and animal breeders. It's important that he stays current in the field by reading journals and reports and by attending scientific meetings. He never seems to have enough time at his desk to do all the paper work that continuously piles up.

A couple days a week, he returns home from a hectic day at the office to put in another couple of hours working in the clinic. Sunday mornings are devoted to performing surgeries and the afternoons to seeing patients. With a schedule like that, he'd have to love his work—and he does.

LESSONS LEARNED

If Blackwell had a chance to do it all over again, there is just one thing he would change. He would have kept his options open as he went through vet school. Instead, he was so sure that he wanted to go into private practice that he didn't give serious thought to other opportunities. Especially in a field like medicine, where there are so many career tracks available, if you don't keep an open mind you might sleep through some great options.

AS EASY AS 1, 2, 3

Blackwell offers three tips for aspiring veterinarians.

1. Be realistic. If your idea of being a vet has only to do with cute, cuddly animals, forget it. Vets often deal with sick and injured animals. You have to be ready to deal with that reality.
2. Get experience working with animals. Find out if you like it and if you can stomach the tough stuff.
3. Work hard and get good grades. Even more important, make sure you really pick up the information you get in your classes (that's called learning). What you are learning now is a foundation for later in life. You'll need a strong foundation to make it through med school.

MAKE A SCIENTIFIC DETOUR!

Science is the foundation for many exciting career paths. This includes up-and-coming opportunities in environmental and technology fields as well as the tried-and-true fields of research, medicine, and the basic hard-core sciences.

It's pretty amazing to think about all the ways you could put your interest in science to work. The following lists include more than 100 scientific careers, and they barely scratch the surface of all the possibilities. These ideas are loosely grouped in categories to help you narrow down specific interest areas. Use them as a starting point to search out the best spot for your scientific interests and abilities.

To make the most of this phase of your exploration, draw up a list of the ideas that you'd like to learn more about. I'll bet there are at least three you've never heard of before. Look them up in a career encyclopedia and get acquainted with more possibilities for your future!

When you come across a particularly intriguing occupation, use the form on pages 133 and 134 to record your discoveries.

$$E = mc^2 \qquad \sqrt{25}$$

A WORLD OF SCIENCE CAREERS

HARD-CORE SCIENCE

This first category lists some of the basic hard-core areas of science. You might be surprised to find introductory courses about these subjects on your list of course options at school. Connect what you are learning in school today with your future!

Also, you'll want to consider the full range of possibilities in each of these areas. Opportunities for technicians start with a strong high school science and math background and technical training and grow from there. In more sophisticated applications of science, advanced education is the key to increased responsibility, opportunity, and income. The following are basic areas of hard-core science.

analytical chemist	geologist	nuclear physicist
biochemist	geophysicist	paleontologist
biologist	microbiologist	petrologist
biotechnologist	mineralogist	physiologist
cell biologist	molecular biologist	physicist
		volcanologist

FRESH AIR, CLEAN WATER, AND OTHER BASIC ESSENTIALS

Growing concerns about issues such as pollution, global warming, wildlife preservation, and energy conservation make the environmental field ripe for scientists who want to make a difference. Many of these opportunities blend a knowledge of scientific principles with a sense of adventure and an interest in working outdoors.

Training requirements vary from job to job. This is an area where summer training programs abound. Get involved and explore all your options.

Environmental Careers Organization
286 Congress Street
Boston, Massachusetts 02210

Environmental Industry Associations
4301 Connecticut Avenue NW, Suite 300
Washington, D.C. 20008

Environmental Protection Agency (EPA)
Headquarters Services Branch
Public Information Center
401 M Street SW
Washington, D.C. 20460
Also check out the EPA's Internet site at http://www.epa.gov.

Here are some specific job titles to check out in detail.

air quality inspector
conservationist
ecologist
environmental
  scientist
fish and game
  warden
forester
forest ranger

hydrologist
inventor of uses
  for recycled
  materials
manufacturer of
  recycled products
park ranger
photovoltaic energy
  researcher

renewable energy
  and energy
  efficiency
  researcher
soil scientist
waste management
wildlife manager
wind energy
  systems engineer

CARING, CURING, AND CONQUERING DISEASE

According to a booklet published by the National Health Council, there are at least 200 ways to put your talent to work in the health field. The following lists some that are especially appropriate for the scientifically minded.

To obtain a copy of the booklet *200 Ways to Put Your Talent to Work in the Health Field* write the National Health Council at 1730 M Street NW, Suite 500, Washington, D.C. 20036-4505. This publication includes highlights of the health-related careers mentioned here as well as many, many more.

In addition, for general information about the medical field you can write to these associations.

American Dental Association
SELECT Program
211 East Chicago Avenue
Chicago, Illinois 60612

American Medical Association
535 North Dearborn Street
Chicago, Illinois 60610

National Dental Association
5506 Connecticut Avenue NW
Washington, D.C. 20015

The following list of medical career ideas includes occupations requiring years of medical school and residency training as well as those requiring short-term or on-the-job training programs. As you consider these options, remember that any job can be the only stop on your career journey (you like it so much that you devote your entire life to it) or the first of many interesting stops. Start somewhere and go from there.

anesthesiologist
audiologist
bacteriologist
blood bank
  specialist
cardiologist
clinical chemist
clinical pathologist
cytogeneticist
cytotechnologist
dental assistant
dental technician
dentist
dermatologist

dietetic technician
EEG technician
endodontist
geneticist
gynecologist
histologic
  technician
licensed practical
  nurse (LPN)
nuclear medicine
  technician
obstetrician
occupational
  therapist

ophthalmologist
optometrist
pediatrician
periodontist
pharmacologist
physical therapist
physician's assistant
podiatrist
radiologist
registered nurse
  (RN)
speech pathologist
surgeon

ON LAND, IN AIR, AT SEA

Oh, the places you can go with a scientific career! Don't overlook the option of working for Uncle Sam in one of the military branches (army, navy, air force, marines, coast

guard); there's great training and opportunity to be found on land, in the air, and at sea.

aeronautical
  technologist
aquaculturist
aquatic chemist
astronaut
aviator
avian veterinarian
cartographist

fishery biologist
geological
  oceanographer
hydrogeologist
hydrologist
ichthyologist
limnologist
marine biologist

marine geochemist
merchant marine
naval architect
navigator
oceanographic
  technician
pilot
ship captain

BUGS, PLANTS, FOOD, AND FURRY THINGS

Work with life in all its forms is represented on this list. Some of these ideas require a full-fledged science education, others require a willingness to work hard and an openness to learn all that nature has to teach.

agricultural
  climatologist
agronomist
beekeeper
biochemist
botanist
cattle rancher

dendrologist
dietitian
edaphologist
ethnobotanist
farmer
hydroponics
  horticulturist

mammalogist
ornithologist
pedologist
silviculturist
viticulturist
zoologist

CRIME, GERMS, AND OTHER MESSY STUFF

You never know what you'll discover in some of these scientific endeavors.

coroner
criminalist
entomologist

epidemiologist
forensic scientist
immunologist

mortician
virologist

A WAY WITH WORDS

Keep your Skill Set in mind as you explore all your options.

health information
specialist
health science librarian

science editor
science journalist
technical writer

A CREATIVE FLAIR

There are ways to combine a range of interests with science.

biophotographer
medical illustrator

science illustrator
underwater filmmaker

STILL SEARCHING FOR THE GREAT IDEA?

After all this, if you're still at that "I know I want to work in science, but I don't know how" stage, a great place to seek out general information is the American Association for the Advancement of Science. Its address is 1200 New York Avenue NW, Washington, D.C. 20005. Make sure you also cruise by the association's Science Next Wave site on the Internet. The on-line address is http://www.nextwave.org.

INFORMATION IS POWER

Mind-boggling, isn't it? There are so many great choices, so many jobs you've never heard of before. How will you ever narrow it down to the perfect spot for you?

First, pinpoint the ideas that sound the most interesting to you. Then, find out all you can about them. As you may have noticed, a similar pattern of information was used for each of the career entries included in this book. Each entry included

- 🔦 a general description or definition of the career
- 🔦 some hands-on projects that give readers a chance to actually experience a job
- 🔦 a list of organizations to contact for more information
- 🔦 an interview with a professional

You can use information like this to help you determine the best career path to pursue. Since there isn't room in one book to profile all these science-related career choices, here's your chance to do it yourself. Flex your scientific muscle by conducting a full investigation into a science career that interests you.

Please Note: If this book does not belong to you, use a separate sheet of paper to record your responses to the following questions.

CAREER TITLE _____

WHAT IS A _____?

Use career encyclopedias and other resources to write a description of this career.

SKILL SET

✔ _____

✔ _____

✔ _____

_____

_____

_____

TRY IT OUT

Write project ideas here. Ask your parents and your teacher to come up with a plan.

_____

_____

_____

CHECK IT OUT

List professional organizations where you can learn more about this profession.

_____

_____

_____

GET ACQUAINTED

Interview a professional in the field and summarize your findings.

_____

_____

_____

DON'T STOP NOW!

GO FOR IT!

It's been a fast-paced trip so far. Take a break, regroup, and look at all the progress you've made.

1st Stop: Self-Discovery
You discovered some personal interests and natural abilities that you can start building a career around.

2nd Stop: Exploration
You've explored an exciting array of career opportunities in science. You're now aware that your career can involve either a heavy-duty dose of science and all the educational requirements it may involve or that it can involve a practical application of scientific methods with a minimum of training and experience.

At this point, you've found a couple (or few) career that really intrigue you. Now it's time to put it all together and do all you can to make an informed, intelligent choice. It's time to move on.

3rd Stop: Experimentation

By the time you finish this section, you'll have reached one of three points in the career planning process.

1. **Green light!** You found it. No need to look any further. This is *the* career for you. (This may happen to a lucky few. Don't worry if it hasn't happened yet for you. This whole process is about exploring options, experimenting with ideas, and, eventually, making the best choice for you.)
2. **Yellow light!** Close, but not quite. You seem to be on the right path but you haven't nailed things down for sure. (This is where many people your age end up, and it's a good place to be. You've learned what it takes to really check things out. Hang in there. Your time will come.
3. **Red light!** Whoa! No doubt about it, this career just isn't for you. (Congratulations! Aren't you glad you found out now and not after you'd spent four years in college preparing for this career? Your next stop: Make a U-turn and start this process over with another career.)

Here's a sneak peek at what you'll be doing in the next section.

☼ First, you'll pick a favorite career idea (or two or three).
☼ Second, you'll snoop around the library to find answers to the 10 things you've just got to know about your future career.
☼ Third, you'll pick up the phone and talk to someone whose career you admire to find out what it's really like.
☼ Fourth, you'll link up with a whole world of great information about your career idea on the Internet (it's easier than you think).
☼ Fifth, you'll go on the job to shadow a professional for a day.

Hang on to your hats and get ready to make tracks!

#1 NARROW DOWN YOUR CHOICES

You've been introduced to quite a few science career ideas. You may also have some ideas of your own to add. Which ones appeal to you the most?

Write your top three choices in the spaces below. (Sorry if this is starting to sound like a broken record, but . . . if this book does not belong to you, write your responses on a separate sheet of paper.)

1. _____
2. _____
3. _____

#2 SNOOP AT THE LIBRARY

Take your list of favorite career ideas, a notebook, and a helpful adult with you to the library. When you get there, go to the reference section and ask the librarian to help you find

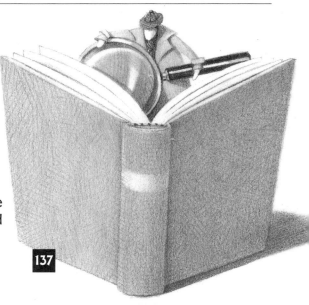

books about careers. Most libraries will have at least one set of career encyclopedias. Some of the larger libraries may also have career information on CD-ROM.

Gather all the information you can and use it to answer the following questions in your notebook about each of the careers on your list. Make sure to ask for help if you get stuck.

TOP 10 THINGS YOU NEED TO KNOW ABOUT YOUR CAREER

1. What kinds of skills does this job require?
2. What kind of training is required? (Compare the options for a high school degree, trade school degree, two-year degree, four-year degree, and advanced degree.)
3. What types of classes do I need to take in high school in order to be accepted into a training program?
4. What are the names of three schools or colleges where I can get the training I need?
5. Are there any apprenticeship or internship opportunities available? If so, where? If not, could I create my own opportunity? How?
6. How much money can I expect to earn as a beginner? How much with more experience?
7. What kinds of places hire people to do this kind of work?
8. What is a typical work environment like? For example, would I work in a busy office, outdoors, or in a laboratory?
9. What are some books and magazines I could read to learn more about this career? Make a list and look for them at your library.
10. Where can I write for more information? Make a list of professional associations.

#3 CHAT ON THE PHONE

Talking to a seasoned professional—someone who experiences the job day in and day out—can be a great way to get the inside story on what a career is all about. Fortunately for you, the experts in any career field can be as close as the nearest telephone.

Sure it can be a bit scary calling up an adult whom you don't know. But, two things are in your favor:

1. They can't see you. The worst thing they can do is hang up on you, so just relax and enjoy the conversation.
2. They'll probably be happy to talk to you about their job. In fact, most people will be flattered that you've called. If you happen to contact someone who seems reluctant to talk, thank them for their time and try someone else.

Here are a few pointers to help make your telephone interview a success.

- ☼ Mind your manners and speak clearly.
- ☼ Be respectful of their time and position.
- ☼ Be prepared with good questions and take notes as you talk.

One more common sense reminder: Be careful about giving out your address and DO NOT arrange to meet anyone you don't know without your parents' supervision.

TRACKING DOWN CAREER EXPERTS

You might be wondering by now how to find someone to interview. Have no fear! It's easy, if you're persistent. All you have to do is ask. Ask the right people and you'll have a great lead in no time.

A few of the people to ask and sources to turn to are

Your parents. They may know someone (or know someone who knows someone) who has just the kind of job you're looking for.

Your friends and neighbors. You might be surprised to find out how many interesting jobs these people have when you start asking them what they (or their parents) do for a living.

Librarians. Since you've already figured out what kinds of companies employ people in your field of interest, the next step is to ask for information about local employers. Although it's a bit cumbersome to use, a big volume called *Contacts Influential* can provide this kind of information.

Professional associations. Call or write to the professional associations you discovered in Activity #1 a few pages back and ask for recommendations.

Chambers of commerce. The local chamber of commerce probably has a directory of employers, their specialties, and their phone numbers. Call the chamber, explain what you are looking for, and give them a chance to help their future workforce.

Newspaper and magazine articles. Find an article about the subject you are interested in. Chances are pretty good that it will mention the name of at least one expert in the field. The article probably won't include the person's phone number (that would be too easy), so you'll have to look for clues. Common clues include the name of the company that they work for, the town that they live in, and if the person is an author, the name of their publisher. Make a few phone calls and track them down (if long distance calls are involved, make sure to get your parents' permission first).

INQUIRING KIDS WANT TO KNOW

Before you make the call, make a list of questions to ask. You'll cover more ground if you focus on using the five w's (and the h) that you've probably heard about in your creative writing classes: Who? What? Where? When? How? and Why? For example,

1. Who do you work for?
2. What is a typical work day like for you?
3. Where can I get some on-the-job experience?
4. When did you become a _____ ?
   (profession)
5. How much can you earn in this profession? (But, remember it's not polite to ask someone how much *he* or *she* earns.)
6. Why did you choose this profession?

One last suggestion: Add a professional (and very classy) touch to the interview process by following up with a thank-you note to the person who took time out of a busy schedule to talk with you.

#4 SURF THE NET

With the Internet, the new information super-highway, charging full steam ahead, you literally have a world of information at your fingertips. The Internet has something for everyone, and it's getting easier to access all the time. An increasing number of libraries and schools are

offering access to the Internet on their computers. In addition, companies such as America Online and CompuServe have made it possible for anyone with a home computer to surf the World Wide Web.

A typical career search will land everything from the latest news on developments in the field and course notes from universities to museum exhibits, interactive games, educational activities, and more. You just can't beat the timeliness or the variety of information available on the Net.

One of the easiest way to track down this information is to use an Internet search engine, such as Yahoo!. Simply type in the topic you are looking for, and in a matter of seconds, you'll have a list of options from around the world. It's fun to browse—you never know what you'll come up with.

To narrow down your search a bit, look for specific websites, forums, or chatrooms that are related to your topic in the following publications:

Hahn, Harley. *The Internet Yellow Pages.* Berkeley, Calif.: Osborne McGraw Hill, 1997.
————. *The World Wide Web Yellow Pages.* Berkeley, Calif.: Osborne McGraw Hill, 1997.

To go on-line at home you may want to compare two of the more popular on-line services: America Online and CompuServe. Please note that there is a monthly subscription fee for using these services. There can also be extra fees attached to specific forums and services, so *make sure you have your parents' OK before you sign up.* For information about America Online call 800-827-6364. For information about CompuServe call 800-848-8990. Both services frequently offer free start-up deals, so shop around.

There are also many other services, depending on where you live. Check your local phone book or ads in local computer magazines for other service options.

Before you link up, keep in mind that many of these sites are geared toward professionals who are already working in a

particular field. Some of the sites can get pretty technical. Just use the experience as a chance to nose around the field, hang out with the people who are tops in the field, and think about whether or not you'd like to be involved in a profession like that.

Specific sites to look for are the following:

Professional associations. Find out about what's happening in the field, conferences, journals, and other helpful tidbits.

Schools that specialize in this area. Many include research tools, introductory courses, and all kinds of interesting information.

Government agencies. Quite a few are going high-tech with lots of helpful resources.

Websites hosted by experts in the field (this seems to be a popular hobby among many professionals). These websites are often as entertaining as they are informative.

If you're not sure where to go, just start clicking around. Sites often link to other sites. You may want to jot down notes about favorite sites. Sometimes you can even print out information that isn't copyright-protected; try the print option and see what happens.

Be prepared: Surfing the Internet can be an addicting habit! There is so much awesome information. It's a fun way to focus on your future.

#5 SHADOW A PROFESSIONAL

Linking up with someone who is gainfully employed in a profession that you want to explore is a great way to find out what a career is like. Following someone around while they are at work is called "shadowing." Try it!

This process involves three steps.

1. Find someone to shadow. Some suggestions include
   - the person you interviewed (if you enjoyed talking with them and feel comfortable about asking them to show you around their workplace)
   - friends and neighbors (you may even be shocked to discover that your parents have interesting jobs)
   - workers at the chamber of commerce may know of mentoring programs available in your area (it's a popular concept, so most larger areas should have something going on)
   - someone at your local School-to-Work office, the local Boy Scouts Explorer program director (this is available to girls too!), or your school guidance counselor
2. Make a date. Call and make an appointment. Find out when is the best time for arrival and departure. Make arrangements with a parent or other respected adult to go with you and get there on time.
3. Keep your ears and eyes open. This is one time when it is OK to be nosy. Ask questions. Notice everything that is happening around you. Ask your host to let you try some of the tasks he or she is doing.

The basic idea of the shadowing experience is to put yourself in the other person's shoes and see how they fit. Imagine yourself having a job like this 10 or 15 years down the road. It's a great way to find out if you are suited for a particular line of work.

BE CAREFUL OUT THERE!

Two cautions must accompany this recommendation. First, remember the stranger danger rules of your childhood. NEVER meet with anyone you don't know without your parents' permission and ALWAYS meet in a supervised situation—at the office or with your parents.

Second, be careful not to overdo it. These people are busy earning a living, so respect their time by limiting your contact and coming prepared with valid questions and background information.

PLAN B

If shadowing opportunities are limited where you live, try one of these approaches for learning the ropes from a professional.

Pen pals. Find a mentor who is willing to share information, send interesting materials, or answer specific questions that come up during your search.

Cyber pals. Go on-line in a forum or chatroom related to your profession. You'll be able to chat with professionals from all over the world.

If you want to get some more on-the-job experience, try one of these approaches.

Volunteer to do the dirty work. Volunteer to work for someone who has a job that interests you for a specified period of time. Do anything—filing, errands, emptying trash cans—that puts you in contact with professionals. Notice every tiny detail about the profession. Listen to the lingo they use in the profession. Watch how they perform their jobs on a day-to-day basis.

Be an apprentice. This centuries-old job training method is making a comeback. Find out if you can set up an official on-the-job training program to gain valuable experi-

ence. Ask professional associations about apprenticeship opportunities. Once again, a School-to-Work program can be a great asset. In many areas, they've established some very interesting career training opportunities.

Hire yourself for the job. Maybe you are simply too young to do much in the way of on-the-job training right now. That's OK. Start learning all you can now and you'll be ready to really wow them when the time is right. Make sure you do all the Try It Out activities included for the career(s) you are most interested in. Use those activities as a starting point for creating other projects that will give you a feel for what the job is like.

WHAT'S NEXT?

Have you carefully worked your way through all of the suggested activities? You haven't tried to sneak past anything, have you? This isn't a place for shortcuts. If you've done the activities, you're ready to decide where you stand with each career idea. So what is it? Green light? See page 150. Yellow light? See page 149. Red light? See page 148. Find the spot that best describes your response to what you've discovered about this career idea and plan your next move.

RED LIGHT

So you've decided this career is definitely not for you—hang in there! The process of elimination is an important one. You've learned some valuable career planning skills; use them to explore other ideas. In the meantime, use the following road map to chart a plan to get beyond this "spinning your wheels" point in the process.

Take a variety of classes at school to expose yourself to new ideas and expand the options. Make a list of courses you want to try.

☼ _____
☼ _____
☼ _____
☼ _____

Get involved in clubs and other after-school activities (like 4-H or Boy Scout Explorer's) to further develop your interests. Write down some that interest you.

☼ _____
☼ _____
☼ _____
☼ _____

Read all you can find about interesting people and their work. Make a list of people you'd like to learn more about.

☼ _____
☼ _____
☼ _____
☼ _____

Keep at it. Time is on your side. Finding the perfect work for you is worth a little effort. Once you've crossed this hurdle, move on to the next pages and continue mapping out a great future.

YELLOW LIGHT

Proceed with caution. While the idea continues to intrigue you, you may wonder if it's the best choice for you. Your concerns are legitimate (listen to that nagging little voice inside!).

Maybe it's the training requirements that intimidate you. Maybe you have concerns about finding a good job once you complete the training. Maybe you wonder if you have what it takes to do the job.

At this point, it's good to remember that there is often more than one way to get somewhere. Check out all the choices and choose the route that's best for you. Use the following road map to move on down the road in your career planning adventure.

Make two lists. On the first, list the things you like most about the career you are currently investigating. On the second, list the things that are most important to you in a future career. Look for similarities on both lists and focus on careers that emphasize these similar key points.

Current Career	Future Career
☼ _____	☼ _____
☼ _____	☼ _____

What are some career ideas that are similar to the one you have in mind? Find out all you can about them. Go back through the exploration process explained on pages 137 to 146 and repeat some of the exercises that were most valuable.

☼ _____
☼ _____
☼ _____
☼ _____

Visit your school counselor and ask him or her which career assessment tools are available through your school. Use these to find out more about your strengths and interests. List the date, time, and place for any assessment tests you plan to take.

_____

_____

_____

_____

What other adults do you know and respect to whom you can talk about your future? They may have ideas that you've never thought of.

_____

_____

_____

_____

What kinds of part-time jobs, volunteer work, or after-school experiences can you look into that will give you a chance to build your skills and test your abilities? Think about how you can tap into these opportunities.

_____

_____

_____

_____

GREEN LIGHT

Yahoo! You are totally turned on to this career idea and ready to do whatever it takes to make it your life's work. Go for it!

Find out what kinds of classes you need to take now to pre-pare for this career. List them here.

_____

_____

_____

_____

What are some on-the-job training possibilities for you to pursue? List the company name, a person to contact and their phone number.

- _____
- _____
- _____
- _____

Find out if there are any internship or apprenticeship opportunities available in this career field. List contacts and phone numbers.

- _____
- _____
- _____
- _____

What kind of education will you need after you graduate from high school? Describe the options.

- _____
- _____
- _____
- _____

No matter what the educational requirements are, the better your grades are during junior and senior high school, the better your chances for the future.

Take a minute to think about some areas that need improvement in your school work. Write your goals for giving it all you've got here.

- _____
- _____
- _____
- _____

Where can you get the training you'll need? Make a list of colleges, technical schools, or vocational programs. Include addresses so that you can write to request a catalog.

- ☼ _____
- ☼ _____
- ☼ _____
- ☼ _____

HOORAY! YOU DID IT!

This has been quite a trip. If someone tries to tell you that this process is easy, don't believe them. Figuring out what you want to do with the rest of your life is heavy stuff, and it should be. If you don't put some thought (and some sweat and hard work) into the process, you'll get stuck with whatever comes your way.

You may not have things planned to a T. Actually, it's probably better if you don't. You'll change some of your ideas as you grow and experience new things. And, you may find an interesting detour or two along the way. That's OK.

The most important thing about beginning this process now is that you've started to dream. You've discovered that you have some unique talents and abilities to share. You've become aware of some of the ways you can use them to make a living—and, perhaps, make a difference in the world.

Whatever you do, don't lose sight of the hopes and dreams you've discovered. You've got your entire future ahead of you. Use it wisely.

SOME FUTURE DESTINATIONS

Wow! You've really made tracks during this whole process. Now that you've gotten this far, you'll want to keep moving forward to a great future. This section will point you toward some useful resources to help you make a totally "on purpose" career choice (that's just the opposite of falling into any old job on a fluke).

IT'S NOT JUST FOR NERDS

The school counselor's office is not just a place where teachers send troublemakers. One of its main purposes is to help students like you make the most of your educational opportunities. Most schools will have a number of useful resources, including career assessment tools (ask about the Self-Directed Search Career Explorer or the COPS Interest Inventory—these are especially useful assessments for people your age). They may also have a stash of books, videos, and other helpful materials.

Make sure no one's looking and sneak into your school counseling office to get some expert advice!

AWESOME INTERNET CAREER RESOURCES

Your parents will be green with envy when they see all the career planning resources you have at your fingertips. Get ready to hear them whine, "But they didn't have all this stuff when I was kid." Make the most of these cyberspace opportunities.

- The Career Center for Teens (a site sponsored by Public Television Outreach) includes activities and information on 21st-century career opportunities. Find it at http://www.pbs.org/jobs/teenindex.html.
- Future Scan includes in-depth profiles on a wide variety of career choices and expert advice from their "Guidance Gurus." Check it out at http://www. futurescan.com.
- Just for fun visit the Jam!z Knowzone Careers page and chat with other kids about your career dreams. You'll find them by going to http://www.jamz.com and clicking on the KnowZone icon. (Behave yourself; it's monitored!)
- JobSmart's Career Guides is another site to explore specific career choices. Look for it at http://www.jobsmart.org/tools/career/spec-car.htm.

IT'S NOT JUST FOR BOYS

Boys and girls alike are encouraged to contact their local version of the Boy Scouts Explorer program. It offers exciting on-the-job training experiences in a variety of professional fields. Look in the white pages of your community phone book for the local Boy Scouts of America program.

MORE CAREER BOOKS ESPECIALLY FOR THE SCIENTIFICALLY INCLINED

Science is a field that offers more opportunity than a single book can contain. Keep looking for the perfect fit for your scientific ambitions. Start with some of the following books.

Czerneda, Julie. *Great Careers for People Interested in Living Things.* Detroit: Gale Research Inc., 1993.

Easton, Thomas A. *Careers in Science.* Indianapolis, IN: JIST, 1990.

Edwards, Lois. *Great Careers for People Interested in the Human Body.* Detroit: Gale Research Inc., 1993.

Grant, Lesley. *Great Careers for People Concerned About the Environment.* Detroit: Gale Research Inc., 1993.

Hawkins, Lori, and Betsy Dowling. *100 Jobs in Technology.* New York: Macmillan, 1996.

Mason, Helen. *Great Careers for People Who Like Being Outdoors.* Detroit: Gale Research Inc., 1993.

Quintana, Debra. *100 Jobs in the Environment.* New York: Macmillan, 1996.

Richardson, Peter, and Bob Richardson. *Great Careers for People Interested in How Things Work.* Detroit: Gale Research Inc., 1993.

———. *Great Careers for People Interested in Math & Computers.* Detroit: Gale Research Inc., 1993.

HEAVY-DUTY RESOURCES

Career encyclopedias provide general information about a lot of professions and can be a great place to start a career search. Those listed here are easy to use and provide useful information about nearly a zillion different jobs. Look for them in the reference section of your local library.

Cosgrove, Holli, ed. *Career Discovery Encyclopedia: 1997 Edition.* Chicago: J. G. Ferguson Publishing Company, 1997.

Encyclopedia of Career Choices for the 1990's. New York: Perigee Books/Putnam Publishing Group, 1992.

Maze, Marilyn, Donald Mayall, and J. Michael Farr. *The Enhanced Guide for Occupational Exploration: Descriptions for the 2,500 Most Important Jobs.* Indianapolis: JIST, 1995.

VGM's Careers Encyclopedia. Lincolnwood, Ill.: VGM Career Books, 1997.

FINDING PLACES TO WORK

Use resources like these to find leads on local businesses, mentors, job shadowing opportunities, and internships. Later, use these same resources to find a great job!

Job Opportunities in Engineering and Technology 1997. Princeton, N.J.: Peterson's, 1996.

LeCompte, Michelle. *Job Hunter's Sourcebook: Where to Find Employment Leads and Other Job Search Resources.* Detroit: Gale Research Inc., 1996.

Also consult the Job Bank series (Holbrook, Mass.: Adams Media Group). Adams publishes separate guides for Atlanta, Seattle, and many major points in between. Ask your local librarian if they have a guide for the biggest city near you.

FINDING PLACES TO PRACTICE JOB SKILLS

An apprenticeship is an official opportunity to learn a specific profession by working side by side with a skilled professional. As a training method, it's as old as the hills, and it's making a comeback in a big way because people are realizing that doing a job is simply the best way to learn a job.

An internship is an official opportunity to gain work experience (paid or unpaid) in an industry of interest. Interns are more likely to be given entry-level tasks but often have the chance to rub elbows with people in key positions within a company. In comparison to an apprenticeship, which offers very detailed training for a specific job, an internship offers a broader look at a particular kind of work environment.

Both are great ways to learn the ropes and stay one step ahead of the competition. Consider it dress rehearsal for the real thing!

Cantrell, Will. *International Internships and Volunteer Programs*. Oakton, Va.: WorldWise Books, 1992.

Guide to Apprenticeship Programs for Non-College Bound Youth. New York: Rosen, 1996.

Hepburn, Diane, ed. *Internships 1997*. Princeton, N.J.: Peterson's, 1997.

Summerfield, Carol J., and Holli Cosgrove, eds. *Ferguson's Guide to Apprenticeship Programs: Traditional and Nontraditional*. Chicago: Ferguson's, 1994.

NO-COLLEGE OCCUPATIONS

Some of you will be relieved to learn that a college degree is not the only route to a satisfying, well-paying career. Whew! If you'd rather skip some of the schooling and get down to work, here are some books you need to consult.

Abrams, Kathleen, S. *Guide to Careers Without College.* Danbury, Conn.: Franklin Watts, 1995.

Corwen, Leonard, *College Not Required!: 100 Great Careers That Don't Require a College Degree.* New York: Macmillan, 1995.

Farr, J. Michael. *America's Top Jobs for People Without College Degrees.* Indianapolis: JIST, 1997.

Jakubiak, J. *Specialty Occupational Outlook: Trade and Technical.* Detroit: Gale Research Inc., 1996.

Schmidt, Peggy. *Careers Without College: Cars.* Princeton, N.J.: Peterson's, 1997.

———. *Careers Without College: Computers.* Princeton, N.J.: Peterson's, 1997.

———. *Careers Without College: Health Care.* Princeton, N.J.: Peterson's, 1997.

Unger, Harlow G. *But What If I Don't Want to Go to College?: A Guide to Successful Careers through Alternative Education.* New York: Facts On File, 1991.

INDEX

Page numbers in **boldface** indicate main articles. Page numbers in *italics* indicate photographs.

A
aerospace engineer 40
agriculture
    chemists 35
    horticulturists 54–55
    veterinarians 120, 121
apprenticeships 145–46, 159
aquariums 87, 89
archaeologist **19–26**
Aristotle 76
artifacts 20
artificial intelligence (AI) 105
associations *See* organizations
  and associations
astronomer **27–39**

B
Basri, Gibor 32–33, *32*
biology-related careers 131
    horticulturist 54–61
    medical technologist 69
    oceanographer 88
    See also health field
biotechnology 49, 54
Blackwell, Dr. Michael 124–25, *124*

blood bank 68, 71
blood testing 68–70
Bonci, Leslie 85–86, *85*

C
cardiopulmonary resuscitation
  (CPR) 71
career options 127–60
    aptitude and interest quizzes
    9–16
    Internet research 141–43
    job titles lists 128–32
    locating/interviewing
      experts 139–41, 143–46
    narrowing down choices
    137–38, 148–52
    no-college options 160
    practice opportunities 159
    research sources 133–34
    training needs 151, 152
CD-ROMs
    astronomy 30
    engineering 44–45
    landscape architecture 64
chemical engineer 40
chemical food analyst 48

chemical medical technologist 68

chemical oceanographer 88, 93–95

chemist **34–39**

civil engineer 40

cloud watching 76–77

competitions
MATHCOUNTS 44
RI/SME Student Robot Contest 107

computer *See also* Internet
as astronomy tool 27, 30
as landscape architecture tool 63
robotics 105, 106, 108

Conte, Anthony 101–4

corn 50–51

cultural anthropology 20

D

Deep Sea Drilling Project 94–95

Department of Agriculture (USDA) 55, 56, 81, 84, 121

Department of Defense 76

dietitian *See* nutritionist

E

electrical engineer 40

Ellick, Carol J. 25–26, *25*

engineer **40–47**
robotics 109–10

environmental careers 128–29
chemists 35
horticulturists 55

landscape architects 62
meteorologists 75
oceanography 89, 91
experiments 35–36, 57, 91–92

F

farming *See* agriculture

Food and Drug Administration (FDA) 120, 124, 125, 126

food scientist **48–53** *See also* nutritionist; veterinarian

Forest Service, U.S. 20, 24

Franklin, Ben 76

G

gardening *See* horticulturist; landscape architect

geological oceanographer 88

Glomar Challenger (ship) 94–95

Greenpeace International 91

H

health field 129–30, 131
medical technologists 68–73
nutritionists 81–83
pharmacists 96–104
veterinarians 119–26

historic preservation 63

horticulturist **54–61**

Hubble Space Telescope 31

I

immunology 69

industrial engineer 41, 46–47

Internet 141–43, 145
archaeology sites 22–23

astronomy sites 30–31
career planning resources 156
chemistry sites 36
environmental sites 129
food science sites 50, 51
horticulture sites 56
medical technology sites 70
meteorology sites 77–78
nutrition sites 84
oceanography sites 90–91
on-line services 142
pharmacy sites 99–100
science education sites 114
Science Next Wave site 132
Science Online Education
  Project (SOL) site 114
search engine 142
veterinarian sites 122
internships 159

J

JETS (Junior Engineering
  Technical Society) 44
Job Bank series 158

K

Kaltenback, Al 93–94, *93*
kitchen chemistry 35–36
kits
  astronomy 29
  chemistry 36
  robotics 108

L

landscape architect **62–67**
Lee, Henry C. 72–73, *72*

Lefebvre, Richard 109–10, *109*
Lindsey, Rose 46–47, *46*
linguistics 20

M

Macaulay, David 40
magazines
  Archaeology 22
  National Geographic 21–22
  Smithsonian 22
  Southern Living 67
management dieticians 81
manufacturing applications
  engineering 41
  food science 49, 53
  robotics 107
materials scientists 35
MATHCOUNTS competitions
  44
mechanical engineer 41
medical technologist **68–73**
medicine-related careers *See*
  health field
metallurgical engineer 41
meteorologist **74–80**
Meteorologica (Aristotle) 76
microbiology 69
military careers 130–31
mining engineer 41
Molner, Ellen 38–39, *38*
Morales, John 79–80, *79*

N

NASA 28, 31, 46
National Agricultural Library
  (USDA) 56

National Marine Fisheries Service Information 91
national observatories 28
National Oceanic and Atmospheric Administration (NOAA) 76
National Weather Service 76
National Junior Horticultural Association (NJHA) 58
natural history museums 19
News for Kids (television program) 116, 117
Nuccio, Julius 60–61
nuclear engineer 41
nurseries (plant) 54, 55, 60–61
nutritionist **81–86** *See also* food scientist

O

oceanographer **87–95**
Odyssey of the Mind (OM) 44
oil drilling *See* petroleum
Olmsted, Frederick Law 62
organizations and associations
  American Association for the Advancement of Science 132
  archaeology 23–24
  astronomy 31
  chemistry 37
  engineering 44, 45
  food science 51
  horticulture 58–59
  landscape architecture 65
  medical technology 71
  meteorology 78
  nutrition 84–85

oceanography 92–93
pharmacy 99, 100–1
robotics technology 108–9
science education 114–15
veterinary 124

P

Page, Ben 66–67, *66*
parks *See* landscape architect
Passport in Time Clearinghouse 23–24
pathologist 70
payload operations director (POD) 46–47
Peace Corps 55
perfumer 38–39
petroleum
  engineer 41
  oceanography 91, 94–95
pharmaceutical chemists 35
pharmacist **96–104**
photosynthesis 56–57
physical anthropology 20
physical meteorology 75
physical oceanography 88
plant-related careers *See* horticulturist; landscape architect
polymer chemists 35
programs
  Boy Scouts Explorer 157
  Odyssey of the Mind (OM) 44
  Project SEED 37
  SEACAMP 90
  TEAMS 44
Project Astro 31

Project SEED 37
public health 120, 125

R
reading suggestions 140,
  157–58, 159, 160
  archaeology 21–22
  astronomy 27
  chemistry 34
  engineering 40, 43
  food science 51
  horticulture 54, 57
  landscape architecture 62,
    65, 67
  meteorology 74, 76, 77
  nutrition 81, 83–84
  oceanography 87, 92, 95
  pharmacy 98–99, 100
  robotics 105
  science education 111
  veterinarian 119, 122–23
robotics technician **105–10**

S
school counselor 156
science careers *See* career
  options; *specific careers*
science educator **111–18**
science fairs 43
science websites *See* Internet
SEACAMP 90
Sea World/Busch Gardens 90,
  91–92
seed catalogs 62
seed companies 55
Socha, Greg 52–53

Space Telescope Science
  Institute 28, 30
Spangler, Steve 115–18, *115*
sports dietitians 81, 86
Squidy (toy) 117–18
Student Robot Contest 107

T
teachers *See* science educator
TEAMS (Tests of Engineering
  Aptitude, Mathematics and
  Science) 44
time capsule 23
TV meteorologist 77, 79–80

U
USDA *See* Department of
  Agriculture

V
Van Cleave, Janice 36
Vaux, Calvert 62
veterinarian **119–26**
veterinary technician 121
videos, robotic 107, 108
volunteer work 145

W
weather forecasting *See*
  meteorologist
weather station 77
WebGarden Factsheet database
  56
Wood, Robert W. 43
World Wide Web *See* Internet
writing careers 132